CONFESSIONS of a RAMBUNCTIOUS KID

A quest for self-discovery and the meaning of life

Written and Illustrated by

JENNIFER LEIGH ALLISON

tree
fort
press

Published by Tree Fort Press

Confessions of a Rambunctious Kid: A Quest for Self-Discovery and the Meaning of Life

Copyright © 2014 by Jennifer Leigh Allison

Library of Congress Control Number: 2014917024

ISBN-13: 978-0-9907712-0-3
ISBN-10: 0990771202

First Edition
Published by Tree Fort Press
Johns Creek, Georgia

www.jenniferleighallison.com

CONTENTS

CHAPTER ONE

My Existential Conundrum

———————◆————————

AS A CHILD, various questions riddled my curious mind all the time. *Why are my eyes green and the sky blue? Why was I born into my family and not someone else's? Why am I here instead of another country or planet? Why now? Does God exist? Why do I exist?*

It didn't seem fair that so many details of my life had been chosen for me without any input of my own. I would have preferred living in a tree with monkeys had I been presented with any options. Given that things were what they were, I began a quest early in life to figure out exactly what my purpose was for being here.

It all started when my mother pushed me into the world at 6:20 p.m. one Sunday. It was the middle of summer on August 18, 1968. It took twelve rigorous hours to usher me in at Princeton Baptist Medical Center in Birmingham, Alabama. I have no recollection of the dramatic event, and I suppose I should be grateful for that. However, my mother remembers the torture vividly. Fortunately, she doesn't hold it against me.

At the time of my arrival, Lyndon B. Johnson was president and The Beatles were entertaining millions of fans around the world. Race riots were erupting throughout the states while our military fought overseas in Vietnam. It was a time marked by political protests and flower power as individuals demanded freedom from social standards by experimenting with free love and mind-altering drugs. My parents were conservative Christians. They didn't condone the newfound hippie lifestyle that had infested pop culture. Their plan was to raise me with strict religious values and do everything they could to protect me from the ungodly society that they believed was destined for hell.

My parents were high school sweethearts who tied the knot soon after they graduated. Their young marriage was one fairy tales are made of until they faced their first trial. The year prior to my birth, Mom miscarried during her tenth week of pregnancy and lost what would have been my older brother or sister. Despite their grief, they eagerly tried again and I became their firstborn. Therefore, they had high expectations that I would bring a lifetime full of joy and happiness, but you know what they say about assuming.

I was trouble from day one. Apart from arriving several weeks earlier than expected, I came out with bright yellow skin, which made me look like a squirming little banana. In order to remedy the jaundice, I had to reside under special fluorescent lamps at the hospital for several days before I was allowed to go home. When I was finally released my excited—but somewhat naïve—parents bundled me up and carried me to our small home in Vestavia Hills.

My father's father, whom I referred to as Papa, told me every time I saw him that he predicted the exact day and time of my birth, only missing it by twenty minutes. That foresight earned him the nickname of Witch by other relatives, but I always loved hearing the story. Somehow it made me feel predestined as though my life was meant to be something special.

My first real memory, other than vague impressions of the patterned wallpaper that hung above my crib as a baby, was when I was eighteen months old. I don't remember why I was running or the impact I shared with the corner edge of a door's frame. I'm also ignorant to the bloody aftermath and the terror my mother expressed when she found me. My first memory begins with the intrusion of intense, white lights hovering just a few inches above my eyes while several faces I didn't recognize struggled to hold me down to a cold, hard table.

As many do, I experienced the childhood rite of passage known as stitches right in the middle of my forehead. The doctor carefully tried to sew my gaping noggin back together as I wiggled and thrashed my little body in defiance. I couldn't understand why my parents wouldn't rescue me as I desperately cried out for help. I was confused by the chaos and ignorant as to why they allowed strangers to poke me in the face with sharp metal objects.

Our brains must record traumatic events with emotional detail because feelings of fear and entrapment are evoked whenever I think about it. Several years later I finally understood the full context of the situation and realized the struggle had been for my best. However, the impression had already been implanted deep inside me that the world could be horrendously cruel and unpredictable at times. This perception became even more of a reality with each year that I grew older.

The first few years of my life were marked by tears—lots and lots of tears. I frequently cried for long periods of time, and for no apparent reason. While it's true that all newborns fuss because it's their only method of communicating, and it's critical to their developing a relationship with their caretaker, I cried an unusual amount.

My parents valiantly spent hours each day as they searched for ways to appease me. They bounced me on their shoulders. They sang to me. My father even took me for car rides around the block because the hum and vibration of the road would settle me down. However, our peace only lasted as long as the engine was running. As soon as we stopped and they attempted to touch me again, then the wailing started all over again.

Eventually my parents sought help at their local pharmacy. There they found a liquid that was popular at the time for colic called paregoric. The magic elixir is described as having a very distinct scent with powdered opium being its primary active ingredient. Mom said it worked like a charm. In fact, it worked so well that I would immediately stop crying as soon as I smelled the bottled drops being opened. I assume that's because of its addictive narcotic properties. Later, she admitted that they depended on it far more than they should have. However, because the federal laws had not yet regulated its use, it was an easy solution. We were all desperate for sleep, and it was the only thing that gave any of us relief.

Despite my crying, Mom was thrilled to have a daughter

she could primp and dress up. Because she was so popular, outgoing, and naturally beautiful, she enjoyed wearing fancy clothes, fixing her hair, and looking pretty with a lot of accessories—even for grocery shopping. In fact, by the time I was born she had owned only one pair of pants in her entire life—always preferring the feminine flair of a dress. She was a girly girl; a child of the '50s, who loved every minute of the poodle skirt era she grew up in.

My mother's mother was a talented seamstress. She could make any style of fabric come to life with ruffles. Therefore, we always had an abundance of custom-made clothes for every occasion. It's not a surprise I became Mom's real life play doll. Bows adorned my head with scotch tape before my hair was even long enough to gather into bands.

Unfortunately, her hopes and dreams of having a prissy little girl all came crashing down! By the time I was a toddler, simply getting dressed was World War III between us. I couldn't bear to feel the seams in my socks or hair in my face. Elastic waistbands and gathered sleeves were especially troublesome. Most fabrics made me itch or feel like my skin was on fire. I tried to communicate through violent tantrums and howls that I was hurting and uncomfortable. Yet my pleas received no compassion. Mom just assumed I needed to learn how to wear clothes, so she persisted with stuffing me into the personal torture chamber.

The only time I wasn't screaming, and yanking on bothersome garb, was when I was allowed to relax in soft, comfortable, cotton pajamas—as long as the tags were cut out. Of course, that wasn't acceptable attire for Sunday school. It became a weekly ritual for my parents to each grab one of my arms and legs and wrestle me into a dress on Sunday mornings. The wrestling didn't stop in my bedroom either. It continued all the way to the car and even down the halls at church. I fought them with every bit of energy I could muster, but I never won.

Dad tried to discipline me for my outrageous behavior, but when I was already lost in a blind fury I barely even noticed his spankings. The discomfort from torturous clothes was actually worse than his slap across my bottom.

Our weekly drama created a lot of puzzling questions in my mind, as well as a distorted worldview at an early age. *Why is church so important? Why must I suffer before going there? Do clothes really make a difference in how much God loves me?*

I was also a picky eater and preferred to stick with a few basics like cheese and crackers. Mom often appealed with me by saying, "What kid doesn't like milk?" All the doctors said it was needed for strong bones and proper growth. Therefore, she believed it was a mandatory requirement to make me drink the nasty stuff. The smell alone was enough to trigger the onset of nausea. Drinking the thick, vanilla yuckiness often resulted in our kitchen looking like a scene from *The Exorcist*.

We always ate dinner as a family, and I wasn't allowed to leave the table until my plate was cleaned. This, of course, was another setup for disaster. With each clank of a fork against a ceramic plate, slurp of tea, or a crunch of ice, my whole body tensed up in defense. I felt like I was going to combust! Instantly, my heart raced and panic flooded over my body. It was extremely unpleasant and not a single mealtime was excluded.

My mother tried giving me the popular speech about

starving children in Africa. However, her appeal assumed my overwhelming feelings could easily be excused by a sense of privilege. It didn't help at all. I simply pleaded in response, "Please send my dinner to the hungry kids. We might be able to save a life, including mine!"

While the rest of my family seemed to enjoy their meals, I cried. I feverishly kicked my legs, with my hands covering both ears, and tried to survive the horrible ordeal. Many times I was left alone at the table while the rest of my family enjoyed their favorite TV shows. This was punishment for refusing to eat like a normal human being. This really added to distorting my self-image.

Am I the only kid on earth who is hurting? Do my parents even like me? Why do they want to hurt me?

Over thirty years later I was diagnosed with sensory processing disorder. SPD means my brain doesn't process incoming sensory data properly. Environmental stimuli can trigger an exaggerated fight-or-flight response without warning. Certain textures and sounds can illicit dramatic responses because my brain interprets the information as a serious life threat. This often results in sudden, and seemingly random, meltdowns when confusion and anxiety consume me. In fact, many things that most people don't even notice can be completely overwhelming for me.

SPD explains many of the everyday struggles I had throughout my life, but unfortunately the diagnoses came too late to help me as a child.

To give you an idea what sensory processing disorder is like, try and imagine how your body would feel if a burglar suddenly entered your home with a weapon drawn. Most likely you would experience a sudden onset of anxiety, while your body filled with adrenalin and your heart raced. Your mind would scramble for ideas, anything, to get out of the life-threatening situation. You would instinctively do whatever you could to stay alive.

My brain responds in a similar way to simple ordinary things: a keyboard typing, a rustling bag of potato chips, a whispered conversation, or even the texture of construction paper or cardboard. I can be perfectly calm and happy one minute, but if somebody walks by wearing flip-flops my entire body will suddenly revolt at the sound of each snap against their heel. My spine will curl with discomfort as jolts of electricity shoot throughout my nervous system. It is not a pleasant experience.

When I'm in a crowd of people at a restaurant, an event, or even at church, I'm probably not engaged in much conversation. I may even appear to be antisocial or unfriendly at times, but that's only because I'm focused on trying to prevent a meltdown. My brain struggles to decipher which conversations are important in a crowd. Without concerted effort, the room full of sounds blend into a nonsensical mess. Many people have joked that I appear to be on Planet Jen a lot —a distant place I go inside my head at times to escape. I guess that's true.

When overwhelmed, my brain immediately kicks into survival mode. If I have no control over the bombarding stimuli, then my heart races at full panic until I'm able to escape. It doesn't matter how many times I tell myself that there's no real threat or that a "normal" person wouldn't be bothered. It still hurts. I guess my brain is a mind of its own.

It's also a strange disorder because some sensory stimuli provoke an involuntary meltdown, but I seem to be underresponsive to other things. For example, sometimes a harmful wound, that should be painful, may go completely unnoticed. I often get bruises or cuts without even being aware of the event that caused it.

There are even some sensations I seek because they make me feel better like spinning around, roller coasters, rocking in a chair, deep pressure massages, or real tight hugs. While a lot of sensory data triggers fight or flight (and most often fight), sometimes I crave more than I'm taking in. As I said, it's pretty strange.

While I was growing up nobody knew that something was actually wrong with me. Neither researchers nor therapists had identified the bizarre disorder yet so everyone just assumed I was an ornery brat.

As a child, I never understood why having a relationship with my parents, and other people, was so difficult. Being in the world only seemed to hurt me, and not them. I was aware there were differences in me, which left me feeling like an outcast. Receiving the diagnoses helped my family put a lot of shattered pieces together and mend years of confusion. However, my childhood felt like an ongoing battle. A battle I never won.

My little brother, Rodney, was born a year after me on October 8, 1969. He was happy, healthy, and easy to care for compared to me. He drank milk, ate whatever food was put in front of him and didn't fight at all about having to wear socks or shoes. I was often asked, "Why can't you be more like your brother?" The unfair comparison only isolated me even more.

How can Rodney enjoy the same things that make me feel like the world is going to collapse on top of me? Is there something wrong with me? Do my parents love him more? Am I broken? Will anybody love me just as I am?

The way most people responded to my differences, which included fights with bullies and constant punishment from parents and teachers, led me to believe I was unlovable. I couldn't figure out how to change myself, and it wasn't for lack of trying. Nor could I understand why I needed to.

Unfortunately, having an undiagnosed sensory disorder was just the beginning of my problems. The underlying struggle became a foundation for other issues to take root and bloom with prickly fruit. My journey to self-discovery was a bumpy road to say the least. It was a road full of potholes and wrong turns, but I learned a lot of valuable life lessons along the way.

Feel free to laugh at my expense while I share my story. Laughter really is the best medicine, and it doesn't have any annoying side effects, unless, of course, you have a funny snort when you chuckle that forces orange juice through your nostrils while you're trying to eat lunch.

Now, if I just had a special uniform and cape to go with my mutant super-human powers I'd be all set, as long as they're made of cotton and the tags are cut out.

CHAPTER TWO

A Curious Mind in a Nonsensical World

———————◆———————

MY INSATIABLE CURIOSITY and inquisitive nature made learning enjoyable for me. Apart from my social awkwardness and trouble sitting still in class, I liked school or at least the books. My teachers seemed to focus primarily on who, what, where, when, and how whenever we studied topics like science and history. However, I was most interested in a different question: why? If my mind became curious about something, it locked in on it like a heat-seeking missile and wouldn't let loose until it became satisfied with a suitable answer.

Every day was a new adventure as I investigated the world around me. I aimed to explore the entire universe: every mountain, jungle, cave, and planet. If the scientists at NASA needed someone to shoot into outer space in a rocket, I was ready to volunteer. The world was my personal playground. Even my own back yard was a completely different world in my imagination.

There was a large tree behind my house that had been struck by lightning years before I got there. The tree wasn't much more than a mangled black stump with a few crispy limbs, but I often wondered what it looked like before its fiery accident. Even though it lacked leaves and had charred bark, I admired the way it reached upwards toward heaven, despite the torture it had endured. Its outstretched arms made me long for heaven myself. The evidence displayed in the tree's affections made me certain that God was up there. I felt lucky to have the dilapidated log in my yard, and I was sure the neighbors were jealous.

My father built a playhouse in the woods near the wounded stump where my brother and I played every day. We pretended like our fort was a massive ship that needed to be defended from oncoming pirate attacks. We found big sticks in the woods to duel each other with as makeshift long swords. It was a lot of fun until I got hit in the eye with flying bark shrapnel.

Once again, my mother rushed me to the doctor for an emergency visit with a head wound. I secretly hoped I had actually earned myself a real eye patch, but I wasn't so lucky. I only got poked in the face by a doctor again, which wasn't any fun at all.

Our house was set on the top of a small hill at the end of a cul-de-sac. My bedroom was at the front end of a long hallway that ultimately led to a bathroom at the other end. From my doorway, I could see straight through a window in the bathroom where another big tree stood in the side yard between our house and the neighbor. At night the tree always morphed into a haggard old lady peering inside the house. She was eager for me to come into the bathroom alone, in the middle of the night, so she could grab me by the throat or ankles. It didn't matter how much I had to pee, if I peeked around my door and saw her twisted face staring back at me, I immediately made a huge leap back into the safety of my blankets. I hoped her long gangly arms wouldn't grab me from underneath my bed either! Sometimes my imagination gets the best of me.

The biggest downside of living in Alabama was the ferocious and frequent tornadoes. I first learned about the violent swirling clouds while watching *The Wizard of Oz* on television. That movie made it very clear that tornadoes were something I wanted to avoid. Although, landing in a more colorful world full of flying monkeys and midgets would have been quite an adventure.

One night during a tumultuous storm, my mother put my brother and me inside the bathtub and covered us with pillows. I'm not sure how much protection a bed pillow would provide if the roof had been torn off, but I guess she deemed it the safest place in our house. She and my father took refuge in their master bedroom closet.

Before long I heard what sounded like freight trains outside our house. While we hunkered down in the tub, I feared the violent noise was really the old tree witch trying to claw her way in through the bathroom window. I tried my best to keep hidden under the pillows with the shower curtain drawn so she couldn't find us. I still remember the overwhelming panic I felt that night. My active imagination definitely made things worse!

We didn't stay in Alabama for long. By the time I was six years old my parents decided to move to Tennessee. They found a beautiful three-acre property with rolling hills out in the country in a new subdivision that was under development. It was located in a small town on the south side of Nashville called Brentwood. It was the perfect location to raise a family, so they decided to build a house for us there.

While our new home was under construction, we took up residence in an apartment complex in Nashville. I marveled at the number of long hallways and endless rows of doors inside the bricked community. There were multiple buildings that sat beside one another, and each was marked with a different giant letter on the outside. We lived inside H, where my brother and I shared a room.

Our new neighborhood was a mysterious labyrinth that I could hardly wait to explore. Any time Rodney and I were able to break free from Mom, we ran from one building to the next, sprinting as fast as we could through the halls of each one.

We ran like monkeys back and forth, everywhere, all the time. I'm pretty sure we annoyed the neighbors as we shouted uproarious battle cries on each mad dash past their doors. However, we were quick to hide whenever someone opened their door and complained. We became experts at ducking into the stairwell and making an emergency exit without being caught. Once we were safe, we always laughed hysterically and dared each other to try it again.

A few months later, our new home in Brentwood was finally ready to move into. We each had our own bedrooms and plenty of space to run around, inside and out. Rodney's room was decorated in red, white, and blue. He had a basketball hoop light hanging from the middle of the ceiling, which was really cool. On the other hand, I wasn't happy at all with my mother's choice of pink and yellow plaid wallpaper, or the flower lamp, hanging in my room.

Why did I get the ugly room? Shouldn't I have been allowed to pick which one I preferred, since I'm the oldest? It's not fair!

Their decision was just more evidence to me, which proved they loved my brother more.

Our front yard had a two large oak trees that stood tall like a couple of giant soldiers protecting our property. Our house sat on top of the first of three hills that made up our rolling property. Behind the house, the land buckled twice more before hitting the dense woods at the top. There were a few evergreen trees positioned in the middle of the third hill so it looked like we had our own Christmas tree farm. It was the perfect landscape for hiking, sledding, and building tree houses.

There were hundreds of acres of woods that surrounded our new house. Blazing trails through the thick forest brush while pretending I was a pioneer was one of my favorite things to do. I often saw snakes, had ticks embedded in my head, and got covered in chigger bites or poison ivy. I didn't care. I loved whacking plants and thorn bushes out of my way in order to reach new undiscovered lands. Sometimes I even placed a stick in the ground with a t-shirt tied to it, or some other personal item, as a way to stake my claim from other people that wandered into the forest as far as I did.

I also loved climbing trees and hiding in the branches behind the camouflage of leaves. That's where I found true peace. Oftentimes, I stayed up there for hours and daydreamed.

What would it be like to live in a tree? What does it feel like to fly? Do birds ever fall?

I just knew the sparrows and owls would be nice neighbors if I could take up residence with them.

The biggest tree in my front yard was a favorite because it had a hollow hole in the trunk where I could hide secret messages for friends that lived nearby. The branches were low to the ground so it was easy to climb too. They were also thick enough that I could lie down and rest comfortably while suspended in the air. I especially loved to hide in that tree whenever we had company coming over. Jumping down and scaring guests as they walked towards our front door was a serious sport to me. I was even more proud of myself if our visitors shrieked at my ninja-like dismount. Dad often reprimanded my shenanigans, but it didn't stop me from trying again.

One memorable day as I walked across the yard to climb my favorite tree, I noticed something, or someone, very peculiar standing beside it. Whoever it was, they were watching me. It made me apprehensive because I had never seen anything, or anyone, like it before.

The bizarre non-human being was as tall as I was, with a bright blue body and skinny legs. It had large creepy eyes that were outlined with bright yellow war paint. A thick colorful robe trailed on the ground for several feet behind him; much like a king would wear. However, instead of being lined with diamonds and jewels, its cape was embedded with dozens of round eyes that carefully watched my every move. It scared me terribly, but it also sparked an intense curiosity that prevented me from running away. Somehow, I felt compelled to walk closer—slowly.

Nervously inching my way towards the creature, I carefully studied every detail of its unusual appearance. When

I got within a few feet, I began to talk to it in a low, gentle whisper. I said, "Who are you? Are you from another planet? Why are you here? Do you need my help?"

Then, in an instant, the beast lifted itself off the ground and took flight with the strangest noise I had ever heard in my life. It sounded like an antique car horn as it blared, "HONK!" I ran to my house as fast as my legs could carry me and frantically screamed, "Mom! Dad! Heeeeeelp!"

I was terrified over the encounter with the unidentified flying object. I couldn't find any words or catch my breath quick enough to explain to my parents what had happened. As I struggled to keep from hyperventilating, I noticed our encyclopedia collection on the bookshelf. I thought it might be able to give me some clues.

After several minutes of frantically turning through the pages of each volume that I grabbed, I eventually found a photo that looked similar to the monster I had seen. It had *Peacock* written underneath it. I went on to read what kind of species it was.

When I finally calmed down enough to communicate, my father laughed at me as I recalled my curious rendezvous. He explained there was a farm nearby that owned peacocks. Apparently one of them escaped and found its way into our yard. He said it was nothing to be afraid of. I thanked God it was just some crazy bird because I genuinely feared that an alien was about to abduct me and take me to outer space!

I was grateful to be safe on planet earth that day, but even more excited that I discovered the awesome set of encyclopedias and their endless amount of fascinating facts. They quickly became my favorite books; my go-to place for every question I had about the world around me. I sat for hours at a time and carefully read through each page of every volume. Different things fascinated me: the Egyptian pyramids, flags of the world, and what each constellation of stars meant in Greek mythology. I spent most of my evenings before bed reading everything I could find. I was a total nerd.

During the day, I spent every minute outdoors. In the south, our long summer days were accompanied by a blistering heat and high humidity, and simply walking outside felt like being bathed in honey. I often altered my clothes by cutting off the legs of my jeans to make shorts. I also made my own tie-dyed t-shirts and removed the sleeves. Being barefoot helped immensely too; not to mention the freedom it gave me from the confinement of uncomfortable shoes.

If nobody else was around to play with, I enjoyed watching the ants march around in the dirt. I was fascinated by their ability to move large breadcrumbs and work as a team carrying them into anthills. I desperately wished I could shrink down and experience the world from their vantage point.

Do they think I'm a giant? I wonder if they're afraid of me. Maybe they think I'm God!

I talked to the ants with gentle words of affirmation and encouraged their hard work, hoping their tiny wiggling antennae wouldn't interpret me as a threat so they wouldn't attempt to hide.

As long as I made it home for dinner at dark, my parents allowed me to play outside all day. If my mother needed me home earlier for some reason she just stood on the porch and rang a large cast iron bell while yelling my name as loudly as she could. We didn't have cell phones back in those days so I was on my own for the most part. I was usually outside from dawn until dusk, and I loved every minute.

Summer nights were even more special. Magic happened when the sun went down and the lightning bugs came out. Our house was far away from the city, so when it got dark it was pitch black. As tiny flickering lights swarmed across our yard, I couldn't tell where the landscape ended and the sky full of stars began. It was remarkable—a truly breathtaking scene. I loved to run around and catch as many of the fireflies as I could. A glass mason jar with nail holes in the top made for a perfect lightening bug home where I could carefully watch the beautiful insects up close.

One night after a successful capture, I laid down in the yard to rest. My glowing glass world sat beside me as I looked up at the sky to search for Orion and Cassiopeia. In that moment, I was filled with awe at the number of glimmering lights. The massive enormity of the universe began to awaken inside me as I gazed up into the heavens.

How far away is the sky? Is there anything past the stars?

With that thought I looked back down at my lightning bug laboratory and back up again.

What if there is someone up there who is looking down at me? What if the stars are really just tiny air holes in the sky so that I can breathe? What if some giant has captured me? Is someone up there studying my every move?

I was suddenly overcome with a powerful awareness of how small I really was; it was an awesome feeling. I gained a whole new perspective on life that night. The universe was a much bigger place than I was able to see. Inherently, I knew that God was real, and I was very excited to be a part of His world.

At this point in my life, I still hadn't been able to answer my biggest question: *Why am I here?* However, I knew the answer was attainable with a lot of research and perhaps a giant telescope.

CHAPTER THREE

Searching for Significance

———◆———

GROWING UP with a hidden sensory disorder meant childhood was full of turmoil and strained relationships without knowing why. I felt awkward around other kids because I seemed to be the only one who was struggling or in trouble all the time. Apparently the world is pretty set on how a kid is supposed to behave at school, church, and home. Unfortunately, I constantly failed to live up to anybody's expectations, no matter how hard I tried.

Getting to church and school on time was a whirlwind of drama every day. I was usually pushed into my classroom with tear track stains on both cheeks, my bottom lip puckered out in a defiant frown, and a deep-seated animosity in my heart. Being forced into the misery of a ruffled dress with tight buckled shoes was a cruel and unusual punishment; one I didn't feel I deserved.

As well as bitter and uncomfortable, I was also dreadfully shy. It was always hard for me to make friends in crowded and overwhelming environments, so I usually sat alone and observed the others. However, sometimes other kids came to class who obviously didn't want to be there either. Their presence gave me a glimmer of hope for friendship since I could relate to them. Slowly, I would gravitate towards them in an awkward attempt to socialize. Sometimes I got lucky and enlisted a new sidekick to participate in various unruly hijinks I was planning. I figured if I was forced to be there, then I would find a way to make it fun.

One week a new girl visited my Sunday school class. She boisterously commanded everyone's attention with loud, funny jokes and defiant behavior. The teacher didn't think she was funny and reprimanded her for disrupting the class. However, I laughed wholeheartedly at her antics. I could relate to being punished a lot, so we became fast friends.

My new friend whispered to me that the communion cups in the sanctuary had wine in them. Then she dared me to drink the leftovers after the service. I wasn't sure what wine was, but by her description it sounded like something fun to try. When church was over, we snuck up and down each row of pews and collected the used communion cups. I drank every last sip we could find. I even pretended like it made me feel dizzy in hopes that she'd like me even more. I didn't realize it was only grape juice, which was the typical practice at a southern Baptist church.

In elementary school I continued with attention seeking shenanigans, hoping to gain the approval of new friends. Wiggling my ears while making silly expressions was a special talent of mine. I performed my goofy facial contortions whenever the teacher had her back turned, which always

caused my classmates to erupt with random
attention made me feel popular, but my teache
the opinion that I was funny. Rather, I got in tro
spent many recess periods inside by myself writing "I pro   e
not to disrupt the class" over and over again on the
chalkboard.

One time my devious deeds couldn't be atoned for in
thirty repetitious lines of chalk, so the assignment was sent
home with me. I had to write, "I will listen to my teacher and
not disturb the class" a hundred times on notebook paper. I
was determined to complete the horrendous task as quickly as
possible so I didn't sacrifice any playtime at home. As a result,
my handwriting was completely ineligible because I forced my
pencil to move as fast as it possibly could. Honestly, a chicken
could have scratched a more readable paper.

When I turned in the assignment the next day, my
teacher was very disappointed with the sloppy attempt. Her
angry eyes cut straight through to my soul. I was paralyzed
into a quiet panic while I waited for my consequences. Finally
she delivered my punishment with one stern word: "Redo!"

I refused to repeat the same monotonous task again, but
I didn't tell her that. Instead, I defiantly erased and rewrote
only a few words here and there to make the paper appear
neater. Of course that didn't fool her at all. She was downright
furious with my deceptive attempt! Overhearing her complain
about me to other teachers added even more fuel to my
animosity towards her. Needless to say, I got to repeat the
assignment for a third time.

By the time spring, summer, and winter breaks rolled
around each year at school, I felt like a piñata that had been
beaten to the point of bursting. I could hardly wait to get

...me to run, climb, and jump! I needed intense physical activity to alleviate the tension and discomfort in my body. If I didn't get sufficient playtime then my inability to sit still in class was made even worse. Time moved slower than a fly in molasses whenever I anticipated school breaks. Patience was just another form of cruel and unusual torture I couldn't bear.

I especially loved the extended winter break during the holidays. I realized at an early age that everyone seemed to be in a much better mood the closer it got to Christmas. I looked forward to those few weeks because I usually squeaked by without too much interference.

My family celebrated Christmas pretty big while I was a kid. First, I received dozens of presents from Santa. Then, the next few days involved opening even more gifts with grandparents and cousins. I received so many new toys that the gigantic pile crowded my room and made it difficult to even play with them all. I had almost everything a child of the seventies could ever want, including an Easy-Bake Oven, an Etch A Sketch, and games like Mouse Trap and Scrabble.

My favorite toys were my action figures like Evel Knievel, the Lone Ranger, and Bionic Woman. However, I was adamantly opposed to ever getting a Barbie and if I ever did, her head immediately became an accessory that might or might not make it back onto her body. I think my disdain for Barbie was simply because I didn't think she could handle rough outdoor adventures with me without crying about a broken nail or getting her hair dirty. Not to mention, I just couldn't bring myself to put her in painfully miserable outfits like ball gowns and high heels.

My parents wanted to give me everything they could for Christmas. I guess they were desperate to see me happy and thought that toys would help. Unfortunately, even nice things couldn't bring long-term healing to my wounded spirit. I really just wanted them to like me, on my terms.

As well as the abundance of gifts, Santa Claus personally visited my house on Christmas Eve. Because other kids didn't get the same kind of visit at their homes, I felt like I had a special relationship with the legendary saint. However, before I could spend quality time with Mr. Kringle it was important to Mom that I was dolled up in a fancy outfit first. She was obsessed with capturing the special moment on camera, so she made sure I looked picture perfect. I hated the discomfort and drama around Santa's visit each year. However, if it meant I got to spend a few private moments with him to ask for the drum set I really wanted, then it was worth an hour of playing Pollyanna for Mom.

Despite the pile of toys Santa always brought, I never got the drums I asked for, year after year. The annual ritual eventually left me frustrated and feeling even more rejected.

Who is this fat guy in a red suit? Does he really care about me? Why does he ask what I want, if he won't get it for me? I did my part by suffering in a dress, but he never comes through!

Easter was the same way with baskets that overflowed with candy and other surprises, as if it were Christmas all over again. As usual, before I could see what the Easter Bunny delivered I had to brush my teeth, comb my hair, and look presentable for pictures. My comfortable astronaut pajamas were apparently not the look my photographer mother was going for. She bought a cute, lacy dress I was forced to change into so she could capture the "Kodak moment" she envisioned. As soon as I had a piece of candy in my mouth, though, I frantically ripped off the annoying garments in protest and yelled at my mother, "How come Rodney is never forced into a scratchy gown? Why do you love him more?"

My mother immediately opposed my assumptions that I wasn't cherished as much as Rodney, but I never believed her. Like they say, actions speak louder than words. He was never wrestled to the ground to have his hair brushed or forced to eat things that made him puke. It was obvious, to me, that I was the object of their wrath.

The Tooth Fairy was my favorite mysterious giver. She didn't bring piles of toys or candy like the others; she brought cold hard cash. However, the nickels and dimes weren't the only reason she ranked number one with me. I had no idea what she looked like, and that allowed my active imagination to run wild with possibilities. I often wondered how she showed up in the middle of the night and desperately wanted to catch a glimpse of her.

Will she come in through a window? Will she float through the ceiling? Will she ride in on some sort of unicorn or trained insect? Is she tiny? Does she have sprinkles on her wings that keep her hovering in place as she carefully zips in to snag my tooth from under my pillow?

The curiosity surrounding the Tooth Fairy's suspicious arrival made me giddy with anticipation. Yet somehow she always managed to sneak in and take my tooth without my knowledge. I found that incredibly impressive.

Whenever I had a loose tooth I wiggled and turned it all day long in hopes it would fall out quickly. I even let my father help with his surefire way to pull a tooth in an instant: by tying one end of floss to my tooth and the other end to a doorknob. My dad was quite the handyman.

One night I took extra care by wrapping my freshly yanked tooth into a special envelope. I drew pictures all over the outside letting the Tooth Fairy know how much I loved her and wanted to see her. I secretly hoped she would give me an extra dime for my creative artwork too. Then I tried to stay awake all night so I wouldn't miss another opportunity to meet her.

When I woke up the next morning, I was immediately upset for falling asleep and missing my big chance. I couldn't believe I had failed again. Even so, I was eager to discover what she had left for me so I scrambled to grab my pillow and see what was there.

Huh? Why is my envelope still here?

I looked inside.

Why is my tooth still here?

I was deeply puzzled and concerned. She had never overlooked me before. I wondered if something horrible had happened to her.

With my stomach in knots I screamed for my parents, "Mom, Dad! Something's wrong!"

Tears gathered in the corners of my eyes as I showed my parents my unclaimed tooth. I whimpered, "I think the Tooth Fairy forgot me."

My parents shared a glance with each other that I was unfamiliar with. It seemed to say, "Uh, oh." Then my mother grabbed my hand and escorted me to the couch. She said she had something very important to tell me.

I was puzzled and frightened over what could have possibly happened to my little pixie friend. Dozens of scenarios flooded my mind, as my mother positioned herself next to me to talk.

That's when Mom and Dad explained that the Tooth Fairy wasn't real. I was shocked. I couldn't quite process what she meant as my hopes and dreams became unraveled in an instant. She went on to say the Tooth Fairy was really just my father and that rattled my thought processes even more.

As understanding slowly crept its way through my mind, I finally connected the dots. That's when the tears began to flow. I questioned her about Santa Claus and the Easter Bunny as well and regrettably learned that they too fell to similar fates.

My world was radically turned inside out and upside down in that moment. My mind raced with a flurry of questions.

Why would everyone lie to me? Why would they go to so much trouble to make me believe their lies? How do I know what's real anymore?

My sadness quickly turned to anger. I jumped up and screamed at my parents, "I hate you! I hate you! I hate you!" I ran to my room, slammed the door, and began a painful grieving process curled up on my bed.

I guess God isn't real either.

Needless to say, by that time in my very young life I felt like I couldn't trust anybody. I was disappointed or angry most of the time. Every day was a major struggle for one reason or another. I began to entertain myself with what seemed to be a brilliant idea: running away. I just knew if I could control my own life that I would finally be happy, so I devised a plan of escape.

My prized possession at the time was a purple Schwinn bicycle with its long white banana seat and flowered wicker basket that hung on the front. The right side handlebar had been upgraded to include a plastic grip that, if twisted quickly, sounded like a motorcycle engine rumbling. It was all I needed to make a swift getaway.

One afternoon after school, I packed everything I could into my bike's little basket—another pair of clothes and a flashlight—and decided to leave. First, I warned my little brother not to tell anybody or I would beat him up. Then, when the coast was clear, I got on my bike and set out to gain freedom and seek high adventure all by myself.

It was not the makings of a great plan. At the ripe old age of seven, I hadn't quite grasped the concept of the future or that there were consequences to the decisions I was making. I was naively confident, at least at first.

The neighborhood I lived in at that time sat next to a large undeveloped field. I decided to travel in that direction. I peddled cautiously and constantly looked over my shoulder to make sure I wasn't being followed.

About thirty minutes later I arrived in the parking lot of our local grocery store. It was there I had my first rational thought.

Uh oh, I forgot to bring food.

I searched my pockets to find I didn't have any money either.

I am such an idiot!

I rode around and looked for dropped coins on the ground and in the ditches along the road by the store. Unfortunately, I didn't find any. I began to criticize myself by screaming, "Now what are you going to do? Where are you going to sleep?"

I couldn't believe I hadn't thought of everything. I sat there for several minutes, straddled on my bike, disappointed with myself. I looked forward to exploring the unknown world, and then remembered where I had come from. This caused an intense internal debate about which way was more advantageous to go. I hung my head, frustrated and unsure of what to do. When I glanced back up towards the grocery store, I felt a rumble of hunger pangs and noticed the increasing dryness that parched my mouth. "Rats!" I cursed myself and headed back towards my house.

On my journey back home I rehearsed random excuses that I would give about why I'd been gone for so long. I was certain to be greeted by two frantic, screaming parents upon my return.

When I finally arrived at the front door my veins pounded with nervousness. I quietly twisted the doorknob and slowly tiptoed in, fully prepared to give my story.

However, when I got inside everything was normal, just like it had been when I left. Mom was cooking dinner in the kitchen, while Rodney watched television with Dad. Nobody even noticed I was gone. Avoiding trouble didn't make me feel any better though. I actually felt worse than I did before. I felt alone—invisible.

My difficult experiences at home, church, and school created a lot of confusion for me. I struggled to fit in anywhere. I felt insignificant, just because I was different. The more I longed to be accepted the way I was, the more disappointed I became. I just couldn't live up to anybody's expectations. Then again, nobody lived up to mine either.

CHAPTER FOUR

Branches and Twigs in the Family Tree

AS A CHILD, spending time with extended family taught me how to seek and develop my specific areas of giftedness. Through them I became inspired to dream and dream big. Their mentoring and influence made me determined to do something great with my life, despite the odds.

My father's parents lived in Birmingham, Alabama, where we always spent our holidays enjoying huge meals together. Mamaw Allison was responsible for preparing our feast, which I actually enjoyed eating. She was also kind, generous, and soft-spoken. She wanted nothing more than to see a smile on my face. She often took my cousins, brother, and I shopping for toys and kept Popsicles stockpiled in the freezer for us. Mamaw even cooked a whole pound of bacon for me one time just because she knew how much I loved it. Her gentle words of affirmation made me feel safe and loved. Her generosity was unmatched by anyone else in my life, because she paid careful attention and gave me things I actually wanted. I longed to have the same kind of gentle spirit she had, instead of the raging chaos that seemed to be mine.

Papa Allison was a gruff, firm man who was a strong authority figure. Being a former US Army drill sergeant, he often delivered short, concise commands whenever I got too rowdy. He made me feel as if I were one of his little soldiers. Even though he scared me into behaving at times, I admired his clear boundaries because I always knew exactly where I stood with him.

He was also a talented craftsman who enjoyed building furniture, toys, and other amazing things out of wood. The few times he allowed me to watch him work, I felt like a special guest inside Santa's workshop. The smell of sawdust was thick in the air, which invigorated my senses with hope and possibility. Watching him shape an old piece of wood into something new was purely magical. His level of expertise and creativity inspired me to pursue my own artistic outlets.

My mother's parents lived in Florida. They were very different from my father's. As a way of distinguishing them from my other grandparents my brother and I fondly referred to them as Mamaw and Papa Beach. They lived just a mile from the white sands and crashing waves in Daytona, where Rodney and I spent many summers playing and building sand castles.

Mamaw Beach was a tiny woman who only stood about four and a half feet tall with shoes on. Papa Beach towered over her at more than six feet. She was a Christian who was active at her church but attended services alone. She was fiery and tough too. One time she told me that she had eyes in the back of her head. I believed her too because I never got away with anything when she was around. Papa always called her Boss and I thought the nickname was endearing. She was very talented with the sewing machine so Rodney and I were often made matching outfits and dressed like twins. Although, he was the lucky one who always got to wear the overalls, while I was stuck with the dress.

Papa Beach was a World War II veteran. Relatives said he was never the same after he came home from the war. He often mumbled racist remarks under his breath and adamantly insisted that the Holocaust and lunar landing were hoaxes. However, he loved watching wrestling on TV and honestly believed they were real. Despite his eccentric and sometimes contradictory behavior, I really loved him. He often took me on long hikes through the backwoods and swamps of Florida, which he referred to as The Boondocks. During that quality time, he taught me about my Cherokee Indian heritage as we searched for animal bones, arrowheads, and civil war relics. He fueled my love for the woods and exploration. Plus, he taught me how to shoot a rifle, which not many nine-year-old girls knew how to do.

As a result of spending so much time with my grandparents, I developed an interest in studying topics like astronomy and archeology in school. The classes were exciting and spawned dreams about a potential career where I could get paid for exploring the universe. I also enjoyed assignments where I got to build things like erecting a tower out of toothpicks or sculpting the solar system out of foam balls. I spent hours perfecting my models. I loved how it felt to work with my hands, just like my grandparents.

One summer day, as a way to overcome sheer boredom, I bought some chicken wire from the hardware store and molded a huge skeleton frame in the shape of a Brontosaurus. It stood several feet tall. I skinned my creature with papier-mâché, paint, and made it as realistic as possible.

My dinosaur was so large it kept getting in everyone's way

around the house. Eventually, my mother asked me to destroy my Paleolithic art. At first I was upset, thinking she didn't appreciate my handiwork. Once I realized my dinosaur was facing extinction, as was the fate of all dinosaurs, it made getting rid of him more fun. Pretending to be a caveman, I went into combat with my giant. I fought it with a baseball bat sword until it was pummeled to shreds in the yard. It was quite a lot of fun.

I developed an artistic flare for making things out of found objects too. Oftentimes rocks and leaves, pieces of trash, and even chewing gum, became mediums to work with. Anything was fair game to become a master work of art.

If it was raining outside and I couldn't go exploring for things to build, I enjoyed taking household objects apart and rebuilding them. Hours were spent deconstructing radios and tape decks just to see what they looked like on the inside. Then I would carefully put each tiny piece back together until it worked again. My curiosity demanded to know how things operated. That kept me occupied and out of trouble, *some* of the time.

I was also an avid collector. My bedroom closest was full of things like a bag of animal skulls, empty coke bottles, and various insects pinned to a board, as well as every *Star Wars* trading card ever made. I was very proud of my collections and added to them whenever I got the chance.

I knew my playthings were different than other girls my age. They had closets full of dolls and stuffed animals and not deceased animal bones. But having tea parties wasn't appealing to me. Being a scientist was more in line with my passions.

I also discovered that my trading cards were great for building massive card houses. Hours were spent meticulously stacking each one to build a paper empire. The thick rough edges made the cards much better building blocks for strong, sturdy structures than slick playing cards. My houses got as high as I could reach while standing on my tippy toes. They were so wide they literally covered the floor in my playroom, which was close to thirty feet long. Once my fortress was complete, I set up action figures like GI Joe, the Bionic Woman, and the Lone Ranger around the perimeter to guard it from enemies; enemies like my little brother who was prone to Godzilla-like behavior.

I also had a growing collection of bottle caps, which were gathered by walking around property lots that were under construction or by making secret excursions to a nearby food mart down the road. I loved spreading my collection out on the floor to count each found treasure. I had a very organized system for counting too.

First, I identified each type of soda or beer cap there was and put them into a horizontal row. Then, each of those caps got a column underneath it of all the duplicate caps, with the best condition ones placed at the top and the most rusted or bent ones at the bottom. I was proud of my display and always on the lookout for new additions.

During one of my expeditions to search for more bottle caps, insects, pebbles, and other random objects to use in crafts or to add to collections, I explored a house that was under construction in my neighborhood. The construction workers weren't present so I had plenty of time to explore without being run off. I found an abundance of nails, wood, and carpet just sitting there unattended.

Look at all this material. I could build an amazing tree house with all of this.

I ran to find a spot in the woods behind my house to build a fort where I could pile up the building materials I needed.

The work of transferring materials to my secret location

was too much for me to handle alone, so I rushed home and persuaded Rodney to help. We took Dad's wheelbarrow and headed back to the construction site to gather as many supplies as we could before sunset. Our treasure was heavy and bulky to transport. This made the effort difficult, and we could only carry a few items at a time. We made numerous trips back and forth. It was an exhaustive ten-acre walk hauling the materials, but I was determined to get what we could while we had the chance; we persevered.

We took two-by-fours and nails on the first few trips, but I needed something sharp to cut off pieces of carpet. I ran home and rummaged through my father's workshop. There I found a knife with a razor blade at the end. After grabbing it, I ran back to meet Rodney, who was guarding our fortune. Then, we cut off a big square of red carpet and smuggled it back to our hiding place.

We spent the next several weeks building our secret fort. Rodney was surprisingly talented with a hammer so it didn't take long before we were able to climb into our makeshift house. I spent a lot of time there, often reflecting on the sins I had committed to make it possible. I knew that stealing materials was wrong, but I hoped nobody would notice. I worried at times about getting caught, but we never did. Unfortunately that led me to believe I was crafty and clever and able to get away with whatever I wanted.

By the time I was ten, I also tried my hand as an entrepreneur. I had accumulated hundreds of stickers over the years (yet another collection), so I decided to convert my stash into cash. Between classes at school I often had a small gathering of kids around my desk as they rummaged through my binder full of decals. I earned an easy three dollars a week by unloading stickers for a dime apiece. I felt rich and important because none of my classmates had jobs yet.

When my sticker collection finally sold out, I moved into candy sales. My mother spotted me with the initial investment needed to buy a box of twelve Goo Goo Clusters. They were my favorite southern candy made with milk chocolate, peanuts, caramel, and marshmallows. Yum! They sold quickly in the school halls, and I doubled my money in no time. I kept a little cash for profit and then used the rest to invest in more boxes. Business was booming. My parents seemed proud of my ability to earn my own spending money.

My favorite assignment in elementary school was a genealogy research project. I interviewed my parents about all of my relatives and then drew a large family tree on a poster board. I wrote down every name, facts about each one, and how they connected to each other. My parents even took me to visit a nursing home in Fort Payne, Alabama, so I could meet my great-grandmother. She was a full-blooded Cherokee Indian and was almost one hundred years old at the time. I was very enthusiastic about meeting her.

When we first arrived at the nursing home, we found my great ancestor lying asleep on her bed. I was disappointed not to interview her for my report. However, the nurse came in and told me a great story that made the visit worthwhile.

In the middle of the night, just a few hours before we arrived, my great-grandmother had gotten out of bed, put a sheet over her head, and walked up and down the halls groaning like a ghost. The nurse went on to say how frightened everyone on staff was because nobody even knew she could walk. She had been lying in bed for years. Not only that, she stood over six feet tall!

The thought of my great-grandmother's long ghostly figure wandering around the halls late at night made me laugh hysterically. A fond admiration swelled inside for her. I was proud to be related to such a humorous and vivacious Cherokee woman. I decided right then that pranks would be a great way to express my creative energy too.

My father continued to research our family's lineage even after my school project was finished. When he discovered our relationship to a famous outlaw from the Wild West, I was thrilled.

My distant cousin Clay Allison was best known for his violent temper, brawling, and involvement in duels and gunfights. He was also known for doing some ridiculous pranks while he was drunk, like shooting himself in the foot while trying to stampede a herd of army mules. He arrived at legendary status after killing thirty-eight people, including a sheriff, then escaping jail by somehow proving the murders were justified. Allegedly, Wyatt Earp was responsible for running him out of Dodge City in 1878, where Clay was terrorizing the town.

After hearing these stories I felt I had a great excuse for getting in trouble and pulling pranks. I had no choice but to be rambunctious. It was in my blood!

My father also discovered that, through marriage, I was related to the famous American frontiersman Davy Crockett, as well the Wright brothers who invented the first airplane. The realization that such enormous amounts of imagination, innovation, and creativity were in my family made me proud to be a part of it. I even felt somewhat lucky to be me.

Spending time with relatives and learning about my family's genealogy birthed an optimistic outlook and hope for my future. I became determined to defy all odds and do something remarkable with my life, just as my ancestors had. Whenever trouble came my way, I remembered where I came from, and it kept me determined to press forward.

When future generations look back into my family history, I want them to be inspired by me just like I was of previous generations. I want them to know the thrill of seeing a vision come to life. Even if that means walking around as a hundred-year-old ghost.

CHAPTER FIVE

My Quarrelsome Indoctrination

———•➤◆◄•———

RIDING THE BUS to elementary school had more than its fair share of challenges for a kid like me who easily went into meltdown mode. Every bounce, bump, and roar of the angry engine, along with the whirlwind of voices from screaming and laughing children, created an intense sensory overload. It was a dreaded daily commute. My neighborhood was the first stop in the morning and the last one coming home in the afternoon. This meant I was trapped inside the chaotic hell-on-wheels for almost an hour, twice a day.

As a survival technique, I always claimed the seat on the last row where I could hunker down safely in the corner to watch everyone else. However, it was impossibly difficult for me to sit still for long; especially if I felt confined and overwhelmed. I usually let negative energy out by jumping back and forth over the seats like a caged monkey.

I also enjoyed devising schemes to make me laugh, like shooting spit-wads at the kids sitting in the front or crawling underneath the seats to tie someone's shoelaces together. I enjoyed watching other kids stumble as they tried to exit the bus. Somehow my shenanigans kept my mind distracted from the flurry of confusion it was in.

One day the bus driver pulled over to the side of the road specifically to warn me to follow the rules—or else. I was supposed to sit still and remain quiet or she would expel me from the bus. Her admonitions didn't intimidate me though. I just took more precautions and carefully watched her eyes in the large round mirror that hung over the driver's seat. Once her glance was fixed on the road ahead, I quickly threw a crumpled piece of paper at someone and ducked behind the seat in front of me. I wasn't as crafty as I thought I was. I got busted, again.

When we arrived at my stop the bus driver informed me that I was not allowed on the bus for the next three days. I could tell she was serious because of the firm tone in her voice and squinted eyes, which were just a few inches from my own. I knew that telling my parents about what happened would lead to even more trouble. Therefore, in an attempt to avoid their consequences, I pretended like nothing happened when I got home that day.

The next morning I walked to the bus stop, just like I did every day, but I hid before I got there and waited for the bus to go by. Once it passed, I walked home and told my father I missed my ride and asked him to take me to school instead. He told me to get in his car quickly and we immediately took off.

My father sped down the road, squealing his tires around every corner. I was surprised at how fast he wanted to get me to school. We even caught up with the bus. To my surprise, when the bus stopped to pick up some kids, he pulled in and parked behind it. Then he instructed me to get out. He said he didn't have time to drive me all the way to school and expected me to board the big yellow nightmare to take me the rest of the way.

My stomach turned with anxiety as I sheepishly grabbed my books. I prayed that the driver wouldn't recognize me. I tried to blend in with the other kids and inconspicuously climb aboard. However, the driver immediately noticed me and said, "Oh no you don't! I told you yesterday. You are not getting back on here for three days." With that she quickly closed the door in my face and drove off while I stood on the side of the road.

My father, ignorant of the truth, was furious and questioned why I had been left behind. I had no words at the moment to lie with, so I confessed. Oddly, rather than drive towards my school, he headed back home. I got excited for a moment, thinking I was going to miss school that day since he didn't have time to take me. When we got home he took off his belt and spanked me instead. He said my punishment was not only because I had misbehaved on the bus, but for lying to him. Then he swiftly drove me to school—with a sore bottom and a bruised ego.

I tried to put my rambunctious ways behind me. I wasn't very successful though. Case in point, there were two older boys who lived in my neighborhood. Like a pair of hungry vultures, they waited by the road for Rodney and me to get home from school every day.

They were a lot bigger than us and as mean as rattlesnakes. They rode their bikes in circles around us and called us names while we walked home from the bus stop every day. They tried everything they could to pick a fight. It didn't bother me to be insulted because I was pretty clever at hurling "Your Mama" comebacks. However, when they started physically pushing my little brother and me around a vicious fire rumbled inside. Enough was enough. They would quickly discover they were messing with the wrong girl!

I devised a plan of retaliation inspired by the Bible. The classic story about David overcoming Goliath was one I had heard a hundred times in Sunday school. I figured if he could beat the mighty warrior with nothing more than a few rocks and a slingshot, then surely I could beat a couple of lame neighborhood bullies the same way.

I roamed around the woods behind my house and carefully collected dozens of sharp, jagged rocks. I created an impressive arsenal of ammunition hidden near my bus stop. I put a few of the scariest looking stones into my backpack and encouraged Rodney to do the same. We were ready for war when the bullies showed up again.

The next day, just as I predicted, our tormentors were waiting for us again. As our bus pulled to a stop, my brother and I got our secret weapons ready in hand. Then, as soon as the bus drove out of sight, we ambushed the bullies by throwing our rocks as hard as we could at them.

Things did not go exactly as planned. I had envisioned the boys running away like little scaredy-cats. I assumed it would be an easy battle given we had the element of surprise. After all, Goliath was defeated after just one blow. Boy was I wrong.

Before I even realized what was happening, the bullies each gathered large handfuls of gravel from the side of the road and hurled them at us with a fierce counter attack.

Hundreds of sharp stone pellets rained down on us. It stung our skin and got dust in our eyes. We were completely caught off guard and there was nothing we could do to protect ourselves. It hurt a lot.

A whole new level of fury and rage boiled inside me. I dropped my books, wiped my face, and put my fists up in the air. With the confidence of a prized fighter I shouted, "I'm going to kill you!"

My threat only made the boys laugh and walk closer. I warned them to stay away, but they persisted. When they grabbed Rodney by the collar I made a snap decision. I grabbed my metal Mickey Mouse lunch box and swung it violently at the head of the larger boy. Unfortunately, at the perfect moment, the bully flinched out of the way. Then Mickey Mouse landed square in the middle of my little brother's face.

Panic rushed throughout my whole body. I growled like a possessed demon. Through gritted teeth I slowly said, "Look. What. You. Made. Me. Do!" I pushed my nemesis out of the way, put my arm around my brother, and walked him home as quickly as I could. They mocked us the entire way.

When we got close to home, Mom saw us coming and ran as fast as she could towards us. The sight of my brother's profusely bleeding face was alarming, to say the least. Her voice was laced with fear. She pulled him away from me and into her arms for comfort and questioned me about what happened.

While gasping for breath, I explained that I hit him with my lunch box. However, I didn't realize how my words sounded when they came out. In the flurry of activity I failed to convey how I was defending him from giants and trying to protect him. She swept my brother away and took him to her car, so they could go to the doctor. As she drove away she yelled at me to stay at home while she went for help because I was grounded.

Why am I in trouble again? I thought I was doing the noble thing!

Once my brother had his facial wound treated at the hospital, my parents decided to do something special, in an effort to change the trajectory of our traumatic day. That evening they went to the planetarium. Not me though. I had to stay home as penance for my crime. For whatever reason, they didn't believe my heroic story once I finally shared the details of our epic battle. I assume it's because I was always picking a fight with Rodney in one way or another.

Anytime something went wrong, I was usually the first to blame since I was the oldest. More often than not, I was actually the true culprit. My parents made every effort to enforce proper behavior, but I was a slow learner or perhaps a bit stubborn. Their methods of discipline varied while they searched for the most effective means of punishment. Since I got in trouble almost every day, they had plenty of opportunities to practice and test a variety of approaches.

My father's primary role in discipline was that of the spanker. He always sported a leather belt, which he could unbuckle and pull into spanking motion with one swift flick of the wrist. It was a convenient tool, since he had easy access to it whenever and wherever I acted out. Many times I was taken to the car during family outings to be taught a lesson.

My mother was never as prepared or accomplished with the art of spanking as my father was. It was more like a Laurel and Hardy routine between us if she tried to discipline me while he was at work. She usually grabbed whatever was nearby in the moment, which included ridiculous things like a spoon, a kaleidoscope, and even a rubber alligator toy. Her attempts to spank me only made me laugh as I mocked her resourcefulness while she chased me around the house. She also tried other ways to get me in line like washing my mouth out with soap and extra chores. One time she even sat on me! It was a valiant effort but failed to work.

Let there be no mistake, my father's spankings hurt. In fact, whenever Rodney got in trouble all Mom had to say was, "Wait until your father gets home." He immediately started behaving in hopes to avoid the pending doom.

I didn't see it that way. Standing my ground was more important to me than the few minutes of pain that would inevitably come; pain I eventually got used to. Besides, whenever they said, "This hurts me more than it hurts you," I really wanted to let them have it by taking on as much of their punishment as I could.

One day my brother and I got into a violent fist fight. It was not unusual for us to get into physical altercations, but this time it was completely out of control. It was so bad it required my father to intervene before one of us was seriously hurt. My father quickly pulled his belt, folded it in half, grabbed each end, and made a loud snap with it. It was a frightening sound that demanded attention whenever he pounced onto the scene.

My father told us we had a choice: we could hug each other, apologize, and say, "I love you," or get a spanking. My brother immediately outstretched his arms towards me and said, "I love you!" However, I kept my arms firmly by my side and tried twisting out of his apologetic embrace. My father insisted that I reciprocate, but I didn't say a word. I crossed my arms and snarled my face in defiance instead.

That day my father gave me what my brother refers to as the worse butt whooping he has ever seen in his life. After each lick across my bottom my father asked if I was ready to apologize and hug my brother, but I always refused. I received about a dozen bright red welts across my bottom before my father finally gave up. Tears may have gathered in the corners of my eyes, but I was proud of myself for not demonstrating false affections.

I tried to do the right thing by staying true to my feelings, but that usually led to more trouble. Shoot, even telling the truth or sticking up for my brother hadn't benefitted me. Noticing the stark contrast between myself and everybody else around me, roots of bitterness took a strong hold deep inside my soul. I figured if everyone assumed the worst from me then they might as well get the worst. Besides, rebellion was much easier.

By the time I was eleven years old, I felt like my life was a cruel game of me vs. everybody else in the world. I was tired of fighting all the time, but I felt like there were no other options. Trouble seemed to be waiting for me everywhere I went. I know I lacked the maturity of personal responsibility in some of my antics, but justice always failed to serve on my behalf. That didn't change anytime soon either.

One afternoon while my grandparents from Florida were visiting, we decided to make a quick trip to the grocery store together. We needed milk and a few other items. My brother and I were actually excited to go too. We hoped to score some candy or at least get the chance to pick out our favorite breakfast cereal. When we finished shopping and walked outside with our bags, I noticed a gray car driving past us that had a t-shirt suspiciously covering the license plate. I was curious and tried to think of possible reasons why someone would do that. I couldn't arrive at a rational conclusion so I just chalked it up as odd, even though I knew something seemed wrong.

A moment later I noticed the same car coming towards us again. This time, without warning, it made a sudden stop right beside us. Then the back door flew open and a young man, about seventeen years old, jumped out. The car squealed its tires and sped around one side of the grocery store, while the young man ran directly towards Mamaw Beach, who lingered a few feet behind me with an armful of bags.

The boy grabbed my grandmother's purse and tried to run. However, the strap was tightly wrapped around her arm. It didn't slip off like he expected so he violently tugged on the purse several times.

I started screaming at the top of my lungs, "Stop it! Stop it!" In a panic, the boy yanked real hard, one last time, and finally got the purse free. Then he took off running around the other side of the building as fast as he could. Without thinking, I started to chase after him with my little brother right beside me.

As we reached the end of the sidewalk in hot pursuit, a police car happened to turn into the parking lot—exactly where the man was running. Rodney and I screamed in unison as loud as we could, "Help!" Fortunately the cop heard us and got out of his car, just in the nick of time. He caught the punk with the purse right as he ran by.

I was amazed at the miraculous intervention. I bent over with my hands on my knees, and gasped for air, as I watched the thief get handcuffed. Instinctively, I praised God for answering my plea for help.

Thank you, God, for sending us a policeman at the perfect time. Thank you! Thank you! Thank you!

When I looked back towards my grandmother, I saw her sitting on the ground holding her arm against her body. A small crowd of people gathered around her. My mom was visibly shaken as well and unsure of what to do. I was shocked and distraught over what had happened. Seeing Mamaw with tears in her eyes wasn't anything I had ever seen before. Bystanders helped her stand up and escorted her to our car. She appeared to be in a lot of pain, which stirred up feelings of panic in me all over again.

Once the policeman had the criminal in the back seat of his car, he came over and asked us questions. We recalled every detail we could for his report. When he was done, we immediately took Mamaw to the hospital.

Adrenaline pumped through my body for a long time after the ordeal. It was very difficult to settle down again. I replayed the situation over and over in my head, wondering if there was any way I could have avoided the incident. I felt personally responsible and cursed myself for not taking precautions or warning my family about the suspicious car when I had the chance.

We spent many long hours waiting at the hospital while doctors took x-rays to assess the damage done to my grandmother's arm. She needed surgery to have metal pins inserted into her bones before a cast could be put on. It was a very stressful day. I repeatedly began telling myself, "Never trust anybody. Always be on the lookout for bad guys. Learn to be a better fighter. And don't carry a purse!"

A few months after the grocery store incident, I started sixth grade. I had become withdrawn in attempt to protect myself from others. I also avoided team activities on the playground during recess and climbed around on the jungle gym instead. I liked to pretend it was a spaceship and even had conversations with my invisible crew as we set out to discover new planets.

I thought I would be good at sports since I worked out a lot at home and was unusually strong for my age, able to lift my body weight on a bench press and do a hundred pull-ups, but nobody else saw me that way. I was always picked last to join kickball or basketball teams, which was humiliating. So I avoided those kinds of games at school whenever possible.

One day our gym teacher announced there was going to be a dodgeball tournament for the entire sixth grade. He said the winner would claim fifty cents as a reward, as well as bragging rights over our school. I desperately wanted that right. I loved the game of dodgeball too, because catching the big red ball meant I would get to throw it as hard as I could at somebody else without getting in trouble for it. So I talked myself into participating in the tournament. I even looked forward to the competition.

On game day our teacher picked the two most popular, athletic boys in our school to be team captains. Then he flipped a coin to see who got to pick their first player. One-by-one they selected their teams. I tried to send telepathic messages as they made their choices.

Please pick me! Please pick me!

More and more kids continued to be chosen while I anxiously stood by and watched.

I tried to move towards the front of the crowd to be

noticed better. I also tried standing in a more confident pose. I even made eye contact with the captains in hopes that they wouldn't overlook me. But as predicted, I was the last one standing there again.

Tension consumed my body. I could hear mumbles of disappointment as I joined the team that eventually got stuck with me. Their mocking made me fiercely determined to win.

I'll show them. They're going to be sorry!

The tournament was held in the school gymnasium where each team started with about forty players on each side. The auditorium filled with raucous chants for each side when the whistle was blown and the game began.

The competition immediately became aggressive and kids were being nailed left and right. Being underestimated as a weak and fragile opponent bought me lots of time through most of the competition because everyone was focused on knocking out the stronger kids first. Strategically, I stayed out of the way as long as I could.

Once the teams were whittled down to about a dozen players each, I couldn't avoid the oncoming attacks any longer. Most of the players left standing at that point were boys who could throw the ball really hard—so hard that the other kids walked off the floor holding on to their bright pink bruises.

All of a sudden a ball came my way; I quickly positioned myself to catch it with confidence.

Yes!

I caught the incoming ball! I couldn't believe it. I had my first small victory taking out an opponent!

Then, by lucky chance, when I threw the ball it caught the ankles of one of my enemy combatants and I got my second victory!

I encouraged myself through the whole event. *Keep it up, Jen. You've got this! You can do it!*

My heart was pounding so hard that I felt every vein in my entire body throbbing. The flurry of sounds, shoes squeaking on the floor and hundreds of screaming voices echoing off the walls, was almost too much to bear. Nonetheless, I fought hard to stay focused. Miraculously, I landed a few more lucky shots until I was finally the last one standing on my team.

There I stood alone, against the team captain on the other side. He confidently held the ball and smiled. I'm sure I looked like scared, rabid animal. Laughter echoed throughout the gymnasium. He acknowledged our cheering classmates with a cocky grin and strutted around his side of the floor. He snickered at me as I positioned myself with outstretched arms and anticipated his assault. The jeers didn't rattle me because I was too intensely focused on the ball. I quietly began to pray.

Oh God, please help me. I need this. Come on God, please. If you are really up there, and you really love me, please help me. I'm tired of being made fun of. I'm tired of always failing. Please God! Help me do this!

The boy finally drew back his arm with a tight grip on the ball and flung it at me as hard as he could. I bent my knees, opened my arms to catch it, and closed my eyes while I prayed one last time for divine intervention.

Then, all of a sudden, I felt the sting of the rubber ball as it blasted against my chest and neck. When I opened my eyes I found the ball clinched in my arms. I was shocked.

I have the ball? I can't believe it. I actually have the ball!

I looked at my opponent whose mouth hung wide open.

He stood frozen and completely astonished at what just happened, while the rest of the room erupted in laughter and applause at my underdog win. It was awesome!

In front of everyone our gym teacher declared me as the winner and gave me two shiny quarters as the promised reward. I felt vindicated. Finally.

It was my proudest moment in my first twelve years of life. In that short moment of victory, I remembered every bully and every naysayer I had met. I felt like I had finally overcome my fears and doubts and proven to world that I was good at something. It was a moment that boosted my confidence and gave me courage to face future adversaries.

Most importantly, I began to realize that God was the only one who really had my back. He never failed to rescue me whenever I called out to Him.

Unfortunately, despite my moment of glory, there were still deep roots of anger, hurt, and bitterness growing inside. I had secrets hidden so deep that my parents weren't aware of them. Secrets so dark I prevented them from even being exposed in my own thoughts. Secrets that festered and spoiled in the depths of my heart. I'll tell you more about that later.

CHAPTER SIX

Tomboy in Toe Shoes

———◆———

I WAS A SKINNY, LANKY GIRL growing up. My long hair was always pulled into a ponytail or tucked under a baseball cap. Mom tried to arrange my hair to flow around my face. That wasn't going to happen though. I immediately pulled it back into a rubber band. Each strand that touched my skin felt like creepy caterpillars were crawling on me with their prickly feet. Even brushing my hair felt brutal to my sensitivities.

I also preferred to wear t-shirts and denim and hated shoes. This was certainly not normal for most girls. Despite my fashion sense, I never understood why it concerned my mother so much that I enjoyed climbing trees and riding skateboards, instead of playing with dolls. She often called me a tomboy whenever she was frustrated at my inability to behave like a normal little girl.

My father, on the other hand, appreciated my natural athletic abilities. He even encouraged me to join a sports team. Fast-pitch softball was popular among other athletic girls, so I decided to try out for the Civitan city league. This was back in the day when kids had to possess the right skills and be drafted to join a team. With that in mind, if I made the cut I would have something to be proud of.

Tryouts were early one Saturday morning and Dad gave me a ride. When we arrived at the field there was a panel of coaches standing in the dirt with their clipboards. They scribbled with pencils as each individual from the long line of girls caught, hit, and threw balls with the man leading the tryouts. I had no idea how I would compare to the others so I was really nervous. When it was finally my turn, I did everything the coaches asked. Even so, at the end of my tryout I was unsure of my performance. I crossed my fingers and hoped to get picked.

Every moment that passed while waiting to find out if I made the team was almost unbearable. Fortunately, a few days later I received the long-awaited call and found out I had been chosen for the green team. Green was my favorite color too. That gave me an extra boost of excitement. I was proud of myself for facing my fear and overcoming the challenge. I hoped that other kids, as well as my parents, would finally see that I was good at something other than making a fool of myself.

Our coach assigned me the position of third base because of my ability to throw harder than the other girls. We practiced hard and eventually won the season with an almost undefeated record. After our last game my coach whispered in my ear, "I just traded two of our girls to another team because their coach drafted you for his team next season, but I wanted to keep you on mine. You are quite a remarkable player." His words astonished me. I had no idea I was that good. His encouragement inspired me to try even harder to affirm his decision to keep me.

For the next several years I played with fierce determination. My hard work was even noticed by other coaches. I always made the all-star team after the regular season was over. I was even asked to join the fast-pitch traveling team in an age bracket two years older. We played in tournaments all over the state and travelled from city to city as a team in a big luxury bus. It was well equipped with numerous beds, a television, and even a bathroom. We usually watched Richard Pryor videos on the way to our games and I loved the laughter and camaraderie. Our team battled to victory many more times than we lost, which made me feel special.

My father was proud of me too. During his youth, he had been voted "Most Athletic" in his senior high school class. He enjoyed having me follow in his footsteps as a ball player. We spent a lot of time together practicing and developing my skills. After every game he took me to the batting cages in Nashville for additional practice. I even enjoyed stepping into the cage marked "Major League" where it threw baseballs at lightning speeds. Miraculously, my little twelve-year-old body was able to make contact and hit the ball. I always drew a crowd of onlookers and reveled in their attention. It felt great to hear strangers telling my dad how amazing his daughter was. In those moments, I was proud to be a tomboy.

My mother, on the other hand, insisted I was too much of a tomboy. She couldn't relate to my enjoyment of playing in the dirt all the time. I was nothing like the prissy little girl she always thought she'd have. She tried signing me up for more graceful activities, in hopes that they would train me to be more ladylike.

I suffered through five treacherous years of ballet lessons. I pleaded with her to let me take Karate instead, but she thought the key to becoming a woman was in the point, plié and pirouette not the roundhouse kick. Leotards and tights were the required attire, which I despised with a passion. They were nothing short of evil. The scratchy fabric made me insane with discomfort.

I complained during every lesson, even screaming with tears while attempting to rip the polyester away from my body. However, Mom was determined that spinning around on my toes and balancing on beams would eventually mold me into a feminine young lady. Many moons and *Swan Lake* dance recitals later, I finally wore her down. She allowed me to quit dancing, but only with the promise to continue with piano lessons instead. I agreed.

Playing piano meant practice—lots and lots of practice. Every day. However, my commitment was lacking, as well as the self-discipline and focus required to succeed. There were too many things I preferred to do with my time, like climbing trees. I'm grateful for the musical theory knowledge I gained during those few years, but my overall attitude only frustrated everyone involved.

One day my piano teacher asked, "Why do you even come to these lessons if you obviously don't want to be here?" I responded, "Please ask my mother this question. It's a very good one."

Between my father's desire to mentor a star athlete and my mother's wishes for a feminine little performer, I became confused about who I really wanted to be. Life was hard enough to make it through a day without a sensory meltdown. The added stress of trying to meet both parents' expectations at the same time was completely overwhelming.

To top things off, I had no safe place to go for refuge. I wasn't even comfortable in my own bedroom at home. Apart from the detestable pink and yellow plaid wallpaper, a painting of a ballerina hung over my bed. Her judgmental eyes followed me around my room and constantly reminded me that I wasn't the little girl my mother wanted. I repeatedly begged my parents to let me paint over the pink walls in red, buy a lava lamp, and hang a poster of Yoda or Garfield to replace the annoying dancer.

After several months of arguing over what colors were appropriate for a girl's bedroom, my parents said they finally made a decision. They wanted to go out to dinner as a family to discuss. Usually a family meeting meant I was in trouble for something, but I crossed my fingers. I remained hopeful to get my wish for a new, improved sanctuary of solace.

As soon as we had our food at the restaurant I enthusiastically asked, "What's the verdict on my room? Can I change it?"

My parents looked at each other briefly, as if to gain confidence for what they were about to tell me. Then, through a sheepish grin, my mother declared, "We have something to tell you."

My heart stopped. I feared the all too familiar trouble that was pending. I clinched my fists in my lap under the table. The smile on her face wasn't fooling me. I just knew they had tricked me somehow, and were about to deliver a painful blow. Then with words I never would have predicted, my mother said, "I'm going to have a baby."

I was excited about the news. I couldn't wait to have another little sidekick for all my wild adventures. However, her announcement didn't quite resolve the question that still obsessed in my mind. It felt like a distraction to the more pressing issue at hand. So I asked, "What does that have to do with decorating my room?"

That's when my mother explained that if she had a girl, the baby would be given my room, and I could move into our extra guest bedroom. But if she had a boy, I'd be sentenced to my pink purgatory for all eternity.

I was thrilled because the other room was much larger and had a king-sized bed in it. It also had plain white walls and green shag carpet. That night fervent prayers went out to the Almighty God of the universe. I literally begged Him to move on my behalf by providing me with a sister.

For the next several months our family debated over names for the baby and what gender it would be. I never ceased praying for God to make a girl. On October 8, 1979, which coincidentally was my brother's tenth birthday, the baby was born. I never have figured out what was so important to my parents in the month of January that they managed to have two kids on the exact same day in October, ten years apart. Then again, Mom and Dad conceiving my siblings is something I really don't want to think about.

Several hours after we arrived at the hospital, my father finally walked into the waiting room where Rodney and I anxiously awaited the news. Then he announced that Deborah Paige Allison was born.

I immediately jumped out of my chair and began to sing, "It's a girl? Woo-hoo! I get a new room. Yay, yay, yay! I get a new room!"

I was grateful to my little sister for the incredible gift she had brought with her—my sacred refuge. Furthermore, I was happy that my mother had another girl, so she wouldn't have to try so hard to change me. Surely my sister could appease her desires to primp and priss.

Nothing succeeded in turning my desires from mud toward makeup. Unfortunately having a little sister didn't take as much attention off of me as I hoped. As a last resort, my mother enrolled me in charm school, which was taught by a former Miss America. The class was full of young girls who were eager to learn about becoming a true southern belle. Then there was me—wearing a baseball cap and a scowl.

For several months Miss America gave her best shot at teaching me how to smile, bat my eyes, and sit up properly in a chair. I even learned how to model on a catwalk. Oh how I despised every minute. During one of our class fashion shows, instead of wearing a fancy gown like the others, I wore my favorite torn-up jeans. I mocked their prissy hip-swinging walk while I made Vanna White hand gestures towards my converse high tops. I thought it was funny, but apparently nobody else did.

The teacher eventually asked my mom to take me out of the class because my rebellious attitude was disruptive. Being expelled from charm school was a badge of honor that I took great pride in. I just wished I had been given a satin sash, like Miss America wore, that said, "Charm School Reject" across it. Then I could strut around and show off my special talent, claiming victory for all the tomboys who struggled to fit in.

I just couldn't conform into someone I wasn't comfortable being. It didn't seem fair that anybody expected me to either.

If God is so great, then why did He mess up so much with me?

CHAPTER SEVEN

My Ungraceful Adolescent Transmutation

TRYING TO DISCOVER who I was meant to be was a puzzle, or mystery, that didn't seem to have many connecting pieces. My conflicting perceptions, which I gathered from parents, teachers, and the crazy world around me, left me scratching my head as to how I fit in. Anywhere. Going through puberty didn't bring any new insights either. In fact, the awkward transition period only amplified my confusion, tenfold.

I first presented my mother with the most dreaded of all life's big questions when I was eight. Without warning, I approached her in the kitchen while she was cooking dinner and asked, "Where do babies come from?"

No doubt my mom was planning to address this kind of question eventually, but she probably assumed it would come a few years later. Obviously, I caught her off guard. She tripped over words and struggled to offer an explanation. Instead she awkwardly pointed towards the bookshelf and said, "There are some books on the shelf over there, if you want to read about it."

I was already quite familiar with the encyclopedia's my mother suggested. As mentioned previously, I often referenced them for questions about life's big mysteries. In fact, my favorite volume was the one marked on the binder with a bright gold letter A. It included a special section in the middle that explained anatomy. Within that section were several thin transparent pages that overlaid a human skeleton underneath. Each layer was an illustration of our body from the inside out. This included bones, organs, muscles, and finally the outer skin. I read the descriptions over and over again. I even cross-referenced other volumes to learn about related diseases and conditions that could affect the various parts of our bodies.

The medical terminology used in the encyclopedia for male and female private parts was especially curious to me. It used much different names than the slang terms I had heard given to them. The outlined drawings also described the unique reproductive functions that each gender was responsible for, but it didn't give the specific insight I was looking for: *How does a baby get into the woman's tummy to begin with?*

I was preoccupied with learning about sex and why boys looked differently from girls. What my mother didn't know at the time was that two years prior to this conversation, I had been exposed to various sexual activities from a neighbor. My experiences were definitely at the root of my curiosity and confusion around the topic.

Back when I was six years old, living in Alabama, there was a seven-year-old girl who lived next door that I really wanted to be friends with. She was often outside turning cartwheels in her yard, which looked like a lot of fun. When I asked my mother if I could go next door to play, she was reluctant to let me out her sight for the first time. However, I begged incessantly until she relented.

When I went next door we didn't turn somersaults as expected. The game my new friend wanted to play was called Strip Show. She taught me several special moves that involved dancing with each item of our clothes before tossing them to the floor. We also explored our naked bodies as we lay on her giant black fuzzy beanbag. One time she snuck me into her parent's bedroom and showed me a closet full of risqué outfits her mother wore when she performed the same kind of dance routines that we rehearsed. She warned me not to touch them though or we'd get in big trouble. We played Strip Show a lot. With music turned up loud, we practiced making our performances just right.

Every now and then other kids came over to play at her house too. We carefully analyzed the differences between our bodies with the boys. One time, my friend's father even enticed me to do some rather unusual activities with another little boy for the reward of a giant colorful sticker. I can vividly remember the cartoon image on that decal he offered. It was the red, white, and blue caped figure known as Bud Man, who promoted Budweiser beer in the seventies. To this day, I can't see a Budweiser commercial without having flashbacks of some of the games we played.

For some reason I never told anybody about the activities that took place next door. When my mother questioned where my panties were one day, I quickly answered with a lie. It must have been a good one too, because she never expressed any concern again. I managed to keep my secrets for over thirty years.

We moved to Nashville about a year later. However, I carried those memories with me. Unfortunately, it wasn't the last time the world taught me some pretty poor life lessons in sexuality.

Once we moved into our new neighborhood in Tennessee, my little brother and I went exploring through the forest behind our house. We hoped to scout out the perfect location for a tree fort. We made it several yards into the woods between our house and another property that was being cleared for construction when I noticed something unusual sitting near the base of a tree. I assumed it was trash one of the homebuilders had left behind because it appeared to be a crumpled old paper bag. Upon closer investigation, it appeared to be some sort of book.

I enthusiastically uncovered it from the muddy leaves and wiped it clean. It was a full color magazine. Each page showed naked people doing really strange things with each other, some of which were similar to the games I had played at my neighbor's house back in Alabama. I wondered why it had been suspiciously hidden in our woods. I decided to keep the treasure we discovered and convinced Rodney to keep it a secret.

For several days the magazine was tucked safely away in my school backpack, until something terrible happened; my mother found it. With an unusual frantic tone, she confronted me about why I had such horrible filth in my bag. She demanded to know where it came from. I explained how I found the book in the woods behind our house, but I don't think she believed me. She was more upset than usual, which made me feel humiliated and embarrassed because I didn't even know what was wrong.

I never saw the picture book again, but the photos were held captive in my mind for several years as I tried to make sense of what they meant. I assumed it was something to be very, very ashamed of. This lesson wasn't the last in my sex education curriculum either.

A couple of years later, the seventies came to a close right as I was completing elementary school. I was excited about the new decade and moving into junior high. However, before we could throw our books into the air and celebrate our sixth grade teachers prepared a final assembly for students. They wanted us to learn about the next phase of our lives, which they referred to as adolescence.

My friends and I whispered in the halls, curious about what wisdom would be imparted to us at the event. It became even more intriguing when they separated the boys and girls into different classrooms for the big talk. The girls were shown a film about how our bodies would be changing soon and what to expect when we got our periods. The video filled me with fear and dread. I began fervently praying to God, begging Him not to let me grow boobs. I couldn't imagine being strapped into an annoying bra every day. All the other girls seemed eager for the changes, but I was terrified. Life was hard enough already.

I did, however, feel the whirl of hormones raging through my body like the film depicted. I was boy-crazy for sure. My cheeks blushed and body rushed with the tingle of excitement if a boy so much as looked in my direction.

There was one boy, in particular, that I liked a lot. His name was Mark. He was shy like me so I was comfortable around him. He sat next to me in one of my classes and shared my interest in drawing cartoons. We wrote hilarious scripts together, full of slapstick humor, for the various characters we created. I developed a big crush on him.

Unfortunately, my relationship with Mark blossomed right as sixth grade was drawing to an end. Knowing my parents wouldn't be supportive of me dating at twelve years old, I feared we were going to be separated over the long summer break. Therefore, I devised a plan to get my brother Rodney to become Mark's friend too. That way it would be more feasible for him to be invited to our house one day.

First, I wrote love letters to Mark every day and Rodney delivered them for me. That helped them get to know each other. Then, I persuaded my brother to ask our parents to let his new friend spend the night. It wasn't long before my master plan came together just perfectly.

I was bubbling with anticipation for my secret date with Mark. When he came over, Rodney and I spent the afternoon showing him our tree house and hiking in the woods. Mark walked next to me on our excursion and I was thrilled. Then, all of a sudden, Mark reached down and held my hand. My arms and legs felt a jolt of electricity run through them as soon as he touched me. It was amazing. The electrifying spark inspired me to come up with another strategy to spend some time with him alone, without my brother.

A secret get-together in the middle of the night—how romantic!

After dinner I slipped Mark a note on a small folded piece of paper. It said, "Meet me in the playroom at midnight. I think we should kiss."

I went to bed around 10:00 p.m. and watched every minute tick by on my clock while I impatiently waited for midnight. When our appointed time grew closer I went to the bathroom to investigate the scene and make sure the coast was clear. My parents were in bed. *Yes!*

With butterflies in my stomach I felt my way around in the dark until I made it to our rendezvous room at the other end of the house.

I wonder if he will show up. Will he kiss me? I'm not even sure what to do. What if I do it wrong?

I waited several minutes for him. Then my anticipation turned to doubt.

This was a bad idea. I bet he doesn't even like me. What was I thinking?

Then, I heard something move in the dark. I whispered, "Hello?"

He answered back, "Where are you? I can't see anything."

I snickered and spoke quietly so he could follow my voice until he found me on the couch. We sat quietly in the darkness for a moment as we fumbled for words. He began by telling me about his favorite *Bugs Bunny* cartoon and we laughed. Then there was another awkward moment of silence. Finally he broke the tension by saying, "I guess we should kiss now."

I agreed and leaned in towards him. He softly put his lips on mine and we held ourselves there for a few seconds.

Hmm…this is awkward, but kind of nice.

All of a sudden, somewhere in the dark shadows behind us, I heard a loud cough and a deep rumbling voice blurt out my name, "Jen!"

It was my father. *Oh, crap!*

I immediately got up, didn't say a word, and ran straight

to my room. I closed the door, got into bed, and scrambled for what to say when I was confronted.

The next morning my father gave me an intense glare with narrowed eyes that let me know exactly how he felt about the situation. It wasn't happy.

Why is a kissing wrong? Is it bad to show affection to boys? What is wrong with me? Dad will kill me if he finds out about the things I did as a little kid!

Everything I had learned or experienced about sex up to this point led me to the conclusion that something was terribly wrong with me. So, I tried my best to suppress the flurry of raging hormones inside as best I could. I was convinced that sex was something I needed to avoid at all cost. Still, this wasn't my last difficult lesson on the topic.

A few weeks later, I started seventh grade in junior high school. It was 1980 and everything was changing with the new decade: everything from my body to the outside world.

Jimmy Carter was president at the time; however, everyone predicted an upcoming change in the oval office because it was almost time to cast votes for a new candidate. There were also drastic changes in the fashion world. Kids traded in their flowers and bellbottoms for large shoulder pads, leg warmers, and big hair. Disco was also dying a slow, imminent death while new forms of music were favored on the airwaves.

I was excited about all the changes and going to a different school. I couldn't wait to have a locker for my books and take science classes that allowed me run chemical experiments and look through microscopes. Despite my trouble in previous years, I hoped for the best with my new start.

Apart from secretly being crazy about boys, science was my favorite class. I even longed to have my own periodic chart of elements hanging in my bedroom so I could study the atomic structures of zirconium, manganese, and all the other precious metals and gases. See, I told you I was a nerd.

My least favorite class was physical education. I enjoyed expelling pent-up energy while playing sports. However, I hated the class because of one particular reason: the locker room where we changed into gym uniforms.

I was extremely shy and insecure with my transforming body. I didn't want to undress in front of anyone. The other girls were confident flaunting what God had given them so far, but I was developing a lot more slowly. I guess my prayers about not wanting boobs had been answered because they were much smaller than anybody else's at the time.

Having other people's eyes on me as I undressed felt like laser beams were burning through my skin with an intense nerve-racking heat. It was worse than dreadful. Therefore, I usually got dressed in a toilet stall or in a more remote area of the locker room where there was more privacy. Sometimes I just lingered around and wasted time until everybody left the room and then got dressed.

One day my gym teacher walked up while I was scrambling into my gym uniform. She asked why I wasn't changing with the others. I looked at the floor and didn't respond. It felt like she was mocking my insecurity. I was embarrassed and desperate to escape the awkward moment. I dressed as quickly as possible and left the locker room.

The rest of the girls in our class waited in the corner of the gym for the teacher to give directions for the day's activity. A huge trampoline had been erected in the middle of the floor where we usually played basketball. We were all excited about learning to bounce and flip.

Once the teacher communicated all the safety rules, she told everyone to stand in a circle around the trampoline and take turns. I could hardly wait to try. However, my turn never came. Instead, the teacher called me over to talk again. Butterflies turned their own somersaults inside my stomach at her request.

She walked me to the far corner of the gymnasium beside her office where she could keep an eye on the trampoline at the opposite end but we had enough privacy to talk without interruptions. She started by saying she had noticed some things about me. Her words immediately made me tense and nervous. I thought she was going to question my insecurity in the locker room again, but the conversation took a turn I never expected.

Without pause or reservation, the gym teacher informed me I was gay. I was completely ignorant to the connotation she was making in her whispered voice. At this point in my life, I had never even heard the word "gay" used that way.

I asked, "Gay? Doesn't that mean happy?"

She corrected me by saying, "No. Not like that. It means a special kind of love—like a man has for a man and a woman has for a woman."

I questioned, "Like brothers or sisters or best friends?"

Unfortunately, that's not what she meant either. As she continued to explain what being gay meant, it eventually donned on me that she was talking about sex. At that moment, my legs became jello. I was unable to stand up straight.

I was completely ignorant as a twelve-year-old about the type of relationship she described. I wasn't even aware there were people in the world like that. I didn't hear another word she said for the next several minutes while she continued to talk. My mind whirled in a chaotic frenzy of questions.

Why does she think I'm gay? Why is she telling me this? Did I do something wrong? Is it because I'm good at sports? Is it because I don't like dresses? What does she want from me? What's going on?

I struggled to decipher her intentions. Completely paralyzed with fear and confusion, I stood there and didn't say another word.

I looked over at the girls by the trampoline, eager to be with them instead. They eventually noticed the terrified look on my face as tears started to roll from my eyes. Finally my teacher put her arm around me and quietly said, "You need to get yourself together and join the group. We'll finish talking about this later."

As I crossed the gym and approached the trampoline, the other girls immediately surrounded me and asked what happened. I wish I hadn't said anything, but my shock and confusion didn't allow for better words. I simply said, "She thinks I'm gay."

Some of the girls started giggling with each other, but a few of them showed compassion. They were curious to know more. Everyone seemed to know what the terminology meant, so I felt even worse for being so naïve. One girl suggested the teacher was gay and tried to make a move on me. Others just pointed and laughed.

I couldn't make eye contact with anybody. I was numb. One girl made an effort to defend me by mocking the teacher.

She gave her a quick wink, then tossed her hair over her shoulder, and blew a kiss at her. However, the look the teacher shot at me once she realized I shared our discussion with the girls made me even more nervous.

Word quickly spread around school about the incident. By the time I got home, my mother had already heard about it from another parent. She tried to comfort me by saying what the teacher had done was wrong. Mom's well-intentioned encouragement only made me feel worse though because I hadn't defended myself. Not to mention, I still struggled to discern the teacher's intentions. Life had presented me with way too many riddles I couldn't solve. Everything came crashing in together like a violent storm inside my head.

The next day my parents met with the school's principal. When he called the gym teacher into their meeting, she denied everything. She even called me a liar. Apparently the principal believed her too. Despite my parent's plea for an investigation, they did nothing to protect me. In fact, I had to stay in the meddlesome teacher's class for the remainder of the school year, humiliated.

I was haunted by the experience every day, terrified that the teacher would hurt me for telling on her. As if that wasn't troubling enough, I was even more humiliated that all my peers were discussing my sexuality. Many of them seemed to trust the judgment of our teacher.

Several days after the incident, I purposefully picked a fight with one of my friends from class. I no longer wanted to associate with anyone who happened to be female. While yelling insults at her in the hallway, I slammed my locker door real loud to draw the attention of people as they walked by. I wanted everyone to see me dissociate from her so nobody would think she was my girlfriend. Yes, it was a cruel and stupid way to deal with my problem. I regret my behavior now. But at that time, isolating myself seemed like the best strategy to allow the rumors to dissipate.

Seventh grade proved to be a disaster of epic proportions. It was contrary to everything I had hoped for. I lost friends instead of making them. I became more withdrawn and self-conscious than ever. I was never invited to school dances or parties. I was lonely and depressed. I simply wanted to disappear into the background and become invisible.

My personal experiences severely confused my self identity, as well as my understanding about sex. This was fertilizer to the roots of bitterness and anger that had already been growing inside. The remaining glimmer of innocence and hope I had as a child was quickly being choked to death by deep, penetrating thorns. Anxiety began to bloom at escalating speeds, and I hadn't even started my period yet.

CHAPTER EIGHT

Social Exchange Theory

————◆————

SOCIAL PSYCHOLOGISTS SAY that human relationships are formed after we carefully evaluate each other. Consciously or not, the hypothesis states that we do a cost-benefit analysis and compare potential relationships with alternatives. They say that self-interest is the central property that drives relationship decisions. From my experience, I tend to agree that most people are simply looking out for themselves. However, self-preservation was really my determining factor in picking friends.

My traumatic childhood, paired with social awkwardness due to an undiagnosed sensory processing disorder, meant I had trouble connecting with others. Being alone was something I enjoyed for the most part. Even so, I still needed to have fun every now and then just to hold my inner demons at bay. My own unique take of the aforementioned theory of social psychologists meant that I carefully chose to be around people who could help me escape and forget my problems with raucous fun and laughter.

As long as I was playing outside, I was happy. I made friends easier and felt much better when I was running wild, without any restrictions. Summer was a healing and rejuvenating season for me that made interacting with people come easier. When it was time for school though, a dark cloud of fear settled in the air above me at all times.

By the time eighth grade started, I was more withdrawn and anti-social than ever. An invisibility cloak would have been my preferred method of survival. Instead, my jacket with the hoodie pulled over my head had to suffice. I actually blended in with the environment pretty well, and went unnoticed by most people, a real nobody. However, hiding in the shadows didn't make me as content as I thought I'd be. I desperately longed for a friend but wasn't sure how to find one.

One day a new girl named Tricia started attending our school. She talked with a funny accent because her family had just moved to our small southern town from the big city of Chicago. Her snarky attitude and quick wit got my attention. She was confidant, outgoing, and didn't care what other people thought about her. She seemed to embody qualities I totally lacked, but admired. I often wondered if we could be friends, but second-guessed myself about asking her to hang out. I laughed at all her jokes and tried hard to be funny myself so that she'd like me.

Later that year, and much to my surprise, Tricia invited me to her fourteenth birthday party. Astonished, I jumped at the opportunity to go. Spending every babysitting dime I had earned, I bought her the coolest presents I could find. I crossed my fingers and hoped she would think I was cool too.

There were about a dozen other girls invited to the party as well, which made me nervous. However, I swallowed my anxiety and went anyways; determined to enjoy myself.

Tricia and I connected immediately. We shared the same sarcastic sense of humor, and spent the whole night boisterously laughing at our own jokes. We even finished each other's sentences, as if we'd been friends for years. Naturally, we became best friends.

Tricia and I started spending all of our time together talking about boys, life challenges, and our hopes and dreams. We watched movies like *The Big Chill, Arthur,* and *Airplane* over and over again and memorized each line. If one of us called out a random quote, then the other could always finish the phrase. We developed so many inside jokes that people around us had no idea what we were talking about. We practically had our own language.

Our friendship quickly became closer than any other I had up to that point. My insecurities seemed to melt away whenever Tricia was with me. I looked forward to starting high school and felt confident about leaving all my bad memories behind since I had a good friend for moral support. But first, Tricia and I had an action-packed summer planned, which started the moment the final bell rang in junior high. It was a glorious bell, which signified the closing, or shall I say opening, of another chapter in our lives.

When the summer of 1982 started, against my mother's wishes, my father bought me a motorcycle: a red Kawasaki KE125. He instructed me not to leave our yard until the odometer reached 500 miles. This was the threshold to prove I knew how to handle the bike. Once the mileage goal was accomplished I gained more freedom as the boundary expanded to include our neighborhood streets. I practiced every day, but you may not be surprised to learn that I often took the motorcycle places I wasn't supposed to go. It was all in an attempt to reach the mileage milestone more quickly.

I didn't have a license to drive on public roads at fourteen, but I didn't care about the law—as long as I didn't get caught. I often snuck the motorcycle out after midnight and rode around with Tricia holding on tight behind me. Somehow the rush of wind in my face helped me escape the frenzied, dark thoughts and feelings that typically consumed me. Plus, I thought the bike gave me a few extra cool points on the social scale. I rode it all over town, even if it was way outside my father's boundaries.

That summer I also met a cute boy at a friend's party. He was very handsome with dark brown hair and olive skin. I was shocked when he expressed an interest in me. My parents were uncomfortable with me dating at fourteen though, so when he asked me out, we had to spend most of our time hanging out my house. Nonetheless, I quickly fell head over heels in love.

My little sister, Debbie, called him Wigum. Only a three-year-old mind would understand why she found the nickname fitting, but I thought it was cute so that's what I called him too. Debbie was always left in the room with Wigum and me as our chaperone. Three may sound a bit young to have the job of watching over two young teenagers in love. However, whenever Wigum tried to kiss me, she demanded our attention back onto her to so we could watch her dance or sing. She was quite good at the job; as my parents predicted she would be.

I enjoyed stealing kisses with Wigum. Making out

seemed to be his favorite thing to do. When I finally had my parent's permission to go to the movies with him, we sat in the back row where our faces stayed glued together for two hours. I guess that's not unusual for a teenage boy. I gladly obliged.

Sometimes Wigum and I rode my motorcycle together into the woods behind my house to get some alone time. Of course, my dad was always outside waiting for us to get back quickly, so we could never stay gone more than a few minutes. It was just enough time to sneak in some more kissing.

One day I was invited to meet Wigum and other friends at the lake for a party. It was the perfect hot day for swimming and lying on rafts in the cold water. After a lot of begging and promising to complete extra chores around the house, my parents finally agreed to let me go. I asked Tricia to come with us as well, so she could meet the boy that was stealing a lot of my time away from her.

Before we left my house that day, I decided to take Tricia for a quick thrill ride on the motorcycle around my neighborhood. I loved to show off on the bike by boosting the throttle to kick up dust and rocks as we climbed the tallest hills. Whenever we were on flat pavement, I gunned the engine and drove as fast as the bike could take us. It was a ton of fun; until it was time to leave for the party.

As we descended a steep dirt road to head back home, I suddenly lost control of the bike as we rounded a sharp ninety-degree turn. Before I even knew what happened, we lost the bike beneath us and found ourselves sliding along the bumpy gravel ground beside it. After body surfing for several painful seconds we fell into a ditch surrounded by boulders and trees on the other side. Then the heavy motorcycle came crashing in on top of me. I was pinned inside the trench.

I tried my best to get up, but was unable to push 300 pounds of hot metal off. I yelled to see if Tricia was trapped as well. Out of nowhere she suddenly appeared above me, then reached down and grabbed the bike. With super-woman strength, she miraculously lifted it up. I scrambled to crawl out from underneath the bike while I had the chance.

I was astonished that we were alive and nothing was broken. As I stood to my feet, I raved about her amazing strength. She was my hero! She gave credit to a powerful adrenalin rush that took over her body when she found me trapped, but I knew I had witnessed a true miracle.

As I dusted off my legs, I was shocked to see a massive burn that covered the inside of my right thigh. Wearing shorts had offered no protection at all. Apparently, the exhaust pipe had been burning its way through my leg until Tricia set me free. Upon realizing the scope of my wound, my thoughts became hysterical. At first, I didn't notice any pain. That was partially due to my own adrenalin rush, and partially because my mind was so distracted as it tried to think of ways to hide the wound from my mother. Besides, I had a very important date at the lake with Wigum that I refused to miss! I decided to suck it up and continue with the day's plans despite the serious injury.

Pain grew as each moment passed, but so did my determination to see Wigum again. He was going on vacation with his family the next day so it was my last chance to see him for the remainder of the summer. Nothing, and I mean nothing, was going to stop me. When my friends at the lake noticed my freshly deformed leg they, understandably, shrieked at its appearance. They also doubted my sanity for not immediately going to a doctor. I brushed it off like it was no big deal and went swimming instead, which wasn't my first dumb idea that day.

By the next day, the throbbing had escalated throughout my body with such intensity I could no longer mask the pain. In fact, I was delirious with the torture. So I finally confessed to my mother. As expected, she totally freaked out. She paused her maniacal episode over my wound long enough to express anger towards my father for buying the bike, then rushed me to the doctor.

The doctor informed us I had very severe third degree burns, which were on the verge of gangrene. This was the result of my reluctance to get immediate help and then soaking in bacteria-filled lake waters. I had compounded the injury exponentially by pretending I was okay. The result of my stubborn ill-advised decision meant I got to spend every day for the next two weeks with the doctor, while he scraped tiny pieces of infected flesh off my wound. It was a long, tedious, excruciating process. My leg hurt for several months following the treatment. I was constantly reminded of what an idiot I was. Ignoring my problem definitely didn't make it go away.

After surviving the summer of 1982, I became a freshman in high school. I took pride in my new school and often went to football games and other school events. I even tried out for the school's softball team, and the coach picked me to continue my tradition at third base. It gave me a boost of confidence to wear the blue and gold uniform that bore the school's name. It didn't matter what temperature it was outside either, I always wore my letterman jacket as an outward symbol to prove that I was good at something.

I was also excited to be in school with my boyfriend. However, Wigum became popular right away and I had doubts about how long our relationship would last. He was a hottie, and I was a total nerd.

After dating for about six months, Wigum wanted to take our relationship to the next level by having sex. However, I was too afraid to make God any angrier with me than He already was. Besides that, I just wasn't interested in the idea. I couldn't understand why he, or any of my friends for that matter, suddenly expressed so much interest in doing it. It seemed totally disgusting to me. Stressful. Wrong. A risk I wasn't emotionally able to take. Unfortunately, we broke up. I was heartbroken.

Tricia made sure I didn't stay down in the dumps for long. She quickly boosted my spirits with a mix tape of our favorite songs from bands like Yes, Journey, Pink Floyd, and Def Leppard.

Music played a huge role in my friendship with Tricia. We went to every concert we could get rides to and always bought matching t-shirts to wear at school next day to prove we had been to the show. There wasn't an easy way to share our favorite songs with each other back in those days so we made mix tapes—which was a fine art in and of itself. If one of us was depressed, then the other recorded a collection of sad songs onto a cassette tape to mourn with. If one of us had a crush on someone, then we made a mix tape of sappy love songs and gave it to the lucky boy we admired. The lyrics could communicate our intimate feelings much better than we could.

Mix tapes were typically constructed by listening to the radio for several days and hitting the record button on a tape deck whenever the DJ announced what song was coming up next. But sometimes it required quick reflexes and nimble fingertips to capture the song when the first note was played. Very careful attention was taken to organize the songs in such a way that they would tell a story. Tricia and I spent many hours creating the perfect soundtracks for various events in our lives.

We also created our own air band with a couple of friends. We practiced every beat of our favorite songs with invisible instruments until we had them down pat. I always pretended to play the drums, as a way to make my childhood dreams come true. Once our musical charades were perfected, we performed in air band competitions at the skate center. We dressed up in zippered parachute pants, checkered Vans, and dark sunglasses for the event. I even wore a tie with piano keys on it. I honestly thought we were cool but looking at pictures of us now makes me laugh and wonder what in the world we were thinking.

Freshman year I made several more close friends: Wendy, Karen, Leslie, Katie, Molly, and Sharon. They quickly joined the ranks with Tricia as my best buddies. I always had someone to hang out with. It was great because I was never left alone to suffer with my dysfunctional, distorted thoughts. My friends were always eager for a new adventure and often supported me with encouraging words.

Because of their friendship, I no longer wanted to be invisible. Instead, I felt invincible. It's true what they say: there is strength in numbers.

CHAPTER NINE

A Precocious Prankster

———————◆———————

AS A TEENAGER, pushing boundaries became my primary objective for fun. I felt compelled, even addicted, to seeing what I could get away with.

Where does this rebellious craving come from? Is it because of my difficult life experiences? Are the infusion of hormones raging through my body responsible? Why can't I sit still? Why do I lie awake all night, thinking of sneaky things to do? Am I evil?

Regardless of the answer, I thrived on putting my clever thinking up against the rest of the world. I aimed to outsmart common sense.

I started out with simple, somewhat innocent pranks. I made more than my fair share of lame telephone calls to random names in the phone book to ask, "Is Mr. Hiney there? I'm looking for Seymour Hiney." Or to ask "Is your toilet running? Then you better go catch it." I even answered my own home phone and if someone asked for Mr. Allison I said,

"Sorry, you can't speak with him. He's buried in the back yard." On Halloween, it was highly likely you'd find eggs thrown at your house or Oreo cookies twisted apart and stuck all over your car.

My mind was constantly racing with devious ideas. So much so, the insomnia became unbearable. I physically couldn't shut my mind off when the rest of the world did. Therefore, the middle of the night became my personal mischievous playground.

Rolling houses with toilet paper with my friends was one of our more common pranks. We were experts in the fine art of TP. Back in the eighties, toilet paper was made in various pastel colors and patterns. We always bought multiple packs in every shade available to ensure the most creative displays. It was a beautiful mess, even if I do say so myself.

We left no bush, mailbox, or branch untouched. I even climbed high into trees, if needed, to ensure the tops were covered well. When a yard appeared to be saturated in paper, we threw even more. Overkill was simply not possible in my mind; more was definitely better!

The hardest part of rolling for us was being quiet. My friends and I could not stop laughing when we tossed our paper grenades into the air. Throwing them as high as we could, we loved to watch them explode into flying streams of tissue. It was a beautiful sight to look up at our finished work in the moonlight while thousands of long, thin sheets flapped gently in the wind. We always drove by our masterpieces the next day too, hoping to find our victims attempting to clean up what we had blessed them with, just for further laughs.

Once we had saturated every neighborhood around town with our display of Charmin art, we grew tired of the same routine. My friends and I longed for new things to do during our late night adventures. I felt driven to do more, and go further, in order to feel the rush of excitement.

Sneaking out of the house was a good way to satisfy the growling adrenalin monster that was growing inside of me. One time when I spent the night with Tricia, we decided to take her parent's car out for a spin in the wee hours of the night. We challenged ourselves with the task just to see if we could get away with it. We strategically agreed that if anybody saw us driving through town, we would pretend like we were sixteen and legal to drive. It wasn't a brilliant plan, but it gave us enough confidence to drive around all night without a license.

Emboldened, we ignored the city curfew that expected kids under eighteen to be home by midnight. We didn't go anywhere special or do anything noteworthy. Yet the thrill of driving when we shouldn't be was enough. We had so much fun that I couldn't wait to try again.

My mother drove a long brown station wagon, which she kept parked in our garage. I wanted to take it for a spin because it provided a much more difficult challenge to take it without getting caught. So one night, I slowly lifted the garage door as quietly as I could. I put the car into neutral and backed it onto the driveway. Once the car was successfully turned around, I was able to coast down the driveway to the road below, where I could start it without being heard. Then I drove through my neighborhood with the headlights off so nobody could see me escape. It was invigorating.

I easily went through the same routine a hundred times or more. I knew exactly what time my parents went to bed and when they woke up. I had roughly seven hours to do whatever I wanted while they slept, peacefully unaware of my nocturnal shenanigans. Every weekend my trips got more outrageous than the last. I drove all over downtown Nashville, Murfreesboro, Franklin, Brentwood, and other nearby cities just to see how far I could go without being caught.

My secret nightlife was so thrilling that I became obsessed with it. The eleven o'clock curfew my parent's had given me didn't matter anymore. If there was a party I wanted to go to, I simply waited for them to go to bed and then snuck out.

One night, around two o'clock in the morning while driving around with my friends Karen and Wendy, a sudden flash of blue lights appeared behind us. When I realized it was a cop, my joy immediately turned into panic. My brain raced with clever ideas to keep us from getting in trouble. I immediately pulled into the subdivision we happened to be passing when the cop got our attention.

I stopped in the first cul-de-sac we passed and the cop pulled in behind me. When he approached my window I immediately rolled it down and greeted him with an angelic smile. He pointed his flashlight at my friends while looking around inside the car.

The cop questioned, "What are you ladies doing out after midnight?"

I responded, "Well, my friend Wendy lives right here," as I pointed at the random house we happened to be parked in front of. "We are spending the night here and needed to run to the grocery store for a few things."

As I heard myself lie to the police officer, I became angry with myself for taking a bad situation and potentially making it worse. I knew it was wrong but couldn't find the self-control needed to stop.

Luckily the cop believed me, or maybe he just thought my friends were cute. Whatever the reason, he didn't interrogate us any further. He didn't even ask for a driver's license. Instead he firmly stated, "Don't let me catch you ladies out here again, okay? It's after city curfew."

We emphatically agreed, then pretended to walk towards the stranger's house until the cop drove out of sight. As soon as he was gone, we jumped back in my car and frantically tried to develop a plan for what to do next.

I was too afraid to drive anywhere else. I knew the police would be watching out for us. Because of the stupid story I had concocted, we needed to wait in my car for daybreak. That would be several long hours, which further jeopardized all of us getting into trouble with our parents later.

About an hour or so into our wait, while my friends and I desperately longed for the comfort of our beds, I suddenly saw the police car turn onto our street again. As he drove towards us I shouted, "Oh no! Quick, hide. He's back!"

We sank into our seats so low we were sitting on the floorboards. The black and white car slowly turned around in the cul-de-sac beside us. Panicked prayers filled the air inside my mom's car. Headlights slowly passed over the top of our heads through the window while we held our breath.

After a few minutes of sheer terror, the cop finally drove away. I couldn't believe we hadn't been discovered; we were barely stooped out of view. However, not getting caught didn't impact me the same way it did Karen and Wendy. They never wanted to be in that situation again. They were mad and desperate for the night to end. However, it fueled my craving to push the boundaries even more. I found it thrilling to almost get caught. Of course, my attitude would destine me for future run-ins with law enforcement.

The most hilarious and gut-wrenching escape I ever made was the night I almost got busted skinny-dipping with Tricia and Karen. One of the crazy things we often did during our middle-of-the-night escapades was to see how many different private pools we could swim naked in. It was almost like we were baptizing ourselves within their sacred chlorine-filled waters. It usually meant we had to sneak into someone's back yard after we crawled through bushes or got past their gate, while they were sleeping. However, if our target was a community pool, it required more acrobatic skills to get over the tall iron fences without being seen.

One particular night we attempted to mark an apartment complex pool off our to-do list. It was about three miles from my house. Tricia and Karen were spending the night with me so we planned on walking the distance once my parents were asleep. My brother usually didn't tag along on my crazy outings but, uncharacteristically, that night he asked to go with us. I can understand why; Tricia and Karen were both cute.

At one o'clock in the morning the four of us walked to the pool and helped each other climb over the tall rod-iron fence to gain access. We were more shy than usual to undress with my brother there. We turned our backs and quickly jumped into the cold water when nobody was looking. Clothes were scattered all over the ground, lawn chairs, and nearby bushes. It was a beautiful, quiet night swimming under the moonlight and glimmering stars.

About fifteen minutes into our peaceful fun, BLAM! The

property lights turned on! This sudden burst of light exposed our naked bodies in the water from every angle. Frantic and paranoid of being caught in our birthday suits, we scrambled as fast as we could to get out of the pool. I yelled, "Meet me in the woods by the road!"

We each grabbed a pile of clothes and streaked as fast as we could to get out of the lights and into the nearby darkness. This involved scaling the fence and running through the complex of buildings to find a safe place to get dressed.

I ran straight for the woods about a hundred yards away. Once I made it, I started to put on the garments I had grabbed. However, I quickly realized they were actually Tricia's clothes and not mine. Unfortunately, her outfit was several sizes too small for me. The shirt was a half shirt that exposed the midriff to begin with, along with tiny shorts. By the time I squeezed into them they barely covered my body and hugged way too tight. I was humiliated, but didn't have other options. I put my shoes on, thank goodness those were actually mine, and prepared to run in case the cops showed up.

After several minutes everyone finally congregated in the woods with me. They laughed hysterically when they saw me half naked in the teeny outfit. However, just as we began to make light of the situation, we saw a policemen turn into the complex. He was not far from where we were standing.

I whispered, "Everybody down! Hide!"

We all ducked behind trees and bushes until the car passed. The cops went straight to the pool and looked around. They drove up and down the streets, obviously looking for us. We watched them for several minutes from our hidden positions behind the tree line until they finally exited the neighborhood.

Even though we escaped capture on the policemen's initial drive by, we still needed to walk down a major roadway to get back to my house without being seen. As suspects on the run, it was a long, scary journey. I knew if the cops saw us we would immediately get busted. It wouldn't take Sherlock Holmes to figure this mystery out; we were the only people out so late at night. Not to mention our wet hair and clothes!

For three very long miles, we hopscotched from one hiding place to another. We stopped and watched for car lights from each of our positions until we felt it was safe to sprint to the next. We hid behind houses, bushes, and crawled inside drainage ditches. Somehow we managed to make our way back to my house unseen, even though we were passed about a dozen times.

When we finally arrived at my house we all fell to the ground and laughed hysterically at our crazy adventure and my ill-fitting clothes. We guessed at what crimes we would have been charged with had we been caught. Trespassing? Indecent exposure? The realizations only made us laugh harder.

The adrenalin rush my body experienced from near misses with law enforcement was powerful. I loved it. It made the discomfort that usually held my senses captive and body feel as if it were under assault, suddenly feel free and exhilarated. I was thriving with pleasure. Like any other kind of junkie I wanted more, so I devised a plan to push the envelope even further.

A new plan came to mind one day when school was canceled because of six inches of snow. Rodney and I built a huge fort in our front yard. We had a stroke of brilliance and packed ice coolers with snow to create giant bricks that formed thick frozen walls. Our square igloo was approximately ten feet wide by four feet tall and very sturdy. We put a piece of plywood on top as a roof and camouflaged it with more snow.

All the neighborhood kids wanted to play inside our fort. We allowed most them to come inside. However, we kept an arsenal of snowballs near the door in case unwanted trespassers or bullies came into our yard.

Later that afternoon, a twelve-year-old boy I didn't know, who had recently moved into the neighborhood, asked if he could come inside. He seemed like a nice kid so I offered him a deal. I said, "If you can bring me the keys to your parent's van at midnight, right here, I will let you play in our fort any time you want."

He was reluctant at first, but I let him peek inside to see how wondrous our snow mansion was. After spending a few minutes convincing him to complete my request, as part of our secret club initiation, he finally agreed. At midnight, he met me with his parent's keys.

It was very peaceful sitting in my fort in the middle of the night. The thick blanket of snow that surrounded me created the most tranquil world I had ever experienced. I sat there quietly and soaked in the silence with my new friend. A few minutes later, I took a long, slow deep breath in and exhaled a cloud of cold white smoky air. It was time to put my dastardly plan into action.

I told the boy I was taking his parents' van for a little while, but I would bring it back soon. I promised him I would never get caught and he wouldn't get in trouble. He apprehensively tried to talk me out of it, but I insisted. I couldn't wait to drive the Chevy van that sat in his driveway. The fact I was only fifteen made my plan exciting. The fact I had never driven a van before, made it even more thrilling. But the fact it was a stranger's vehicle I'd be stealing, it made the rush incredibly potent.

The van was parked at the top of a long and winding driveway, covered in ice. I decided to start the ignition where it was, rather than pushing it to the road like I did with my mother's car. I was willing to gamble they wouldn't hear the engine start since their bedrooms were on the opposite side of the house.

Once I had the van in my possession, I carefully drove it all over town. I even picked up friends along the way, for the ultimate joyriding adventure. My heart pounded with excitement as I slowly blazed a trail through snow-covered roads without a license.

I knew I would go to prison for grand theft auto if I got caught. My life would be over, as I knew it, if I wrecked or swerved off the icy roads or got their van stuck somewhere. However, the long list of things that could go wrong somehow inspired me to continue. With confidence I drove around for several hours that night proving, to no one other than myself, that I was clever.

When I finally headed back to return the van, the adrenalin kicked in even more. I feared that the neighbors had noticed their van was gone and police would be waiting for me. Fortunately, when I arrived everything was still quiet and dark but I needed to successfully park the van in the exact same position it was before, without being seen or heard. I hoped enough snow would continue to fall to cover my tracks up and down their driveway.

I safely maneuvered the vehicle back to its original position and left the keys where my young accomplice could find them the next morning. Then I ran back home. When I finally climbed into bed, I wondered what drove me to such extremes for fun. I knew it wasn't right, but I felt compelled to do crazy things since I was able to get away with it.

By the time I was legally old enough to drive, the thrill of sneaking out had lost some of its thrill. So, I looked for other ways to get the adrenalin fix I needed.

There was a rumor amongst my school peers about an old satanic church hidden in the woods. Devil worshippers allegedly gathered there on certain nights, sacrificed bodies, and performed other evil rituals. As soon as I heard the story I wanted to investigate and see if it was true. So naturally, in wee hours of the night, I talked my friends Tricia and Karen into going with me to explore.

As we pulled onto a dirt road, overgrown with thorns and weeds, we began to feel nervous and uncertain. Karen wasn't as fearless as Tricia and I, or perhaps she was just a lot wiser and more mature. She begged me to turn around and leave. Regardless of her pleas, I was determined to find out if the rumors were true so I kept going.

After a minute of slowly driving through the creepy woods, the headlights of my car revealed a run-down structure. This mystery building was camouflaged inside the trees, exactly as it had been described. Karen insisted, "We should leave! We should leave right now!"

My heart began thumping so loud inside my chest that I could hear each beat vibrate inside my ears. We quietly got out of my car with our flashlights. The three of us held each other tightly as we walked along the nightmarish trail to explore the devil's sanctuary.

In the black darkness ahead of us was an old abandoned building that barely stood in ruins. It no longer had a roof. Only three of the walls were still standing, which were made from large gray stones botched together with sloppy piles of cement. The fourth wall lay demolished on the ground as a huge pile of rubble. It was difficult to walk around on the floor of debris. There were large rectangular holes in one of the walls—holes where windows once existed—which left a good space for us to stand as we looked down into the center of the structure.

A large red pentagram was painted on one wall and praises to Satan on the others. We quietly discussed the alleged ceremonies that took place there as we scanned the scene with our dim flashlights. As we stood in the chilling chapel we all became overwhelmed with an unnerving sensation that we were being watched. We agreed to leave after only a few minutes of scouting. It was just too creepy!

As soon as we got back to my car, I sped down the unpaved road as fast as I could. I was genuinely scared, but the trepidation was stimulating.

We revisited the eerie church on numerous occasions. I enjoyed taking new friends there for a scare. I dramatically shared the rumors about satanic liturgies that took place as I drove there each time. It was always a terrifying experience to explore the menacing temple, especially under a full moon.

For most people getting in trouble with their parents, or the law, or demonic spirits would serve as a good warning and they would correct their behavior. Not for me; it didn't seem to help. The thrill that came with successfully overcoming peril was so great that I looked for even more dangerous things to do. I was addicted to the pleasurable adrenalin rush it gave me. I just couldn't help myself. At times there was a rational, moral voice inside that warned me about the impending doom I'd face for my sins, but I convinced myself not to listen.

Why does feeling good have to be so bad? If it makes me happy, and nobody gets hurt, then who cares?

CHAPTER TEN

Mary Jane and Me

———————◆———————

THE SKATE CENTER was a regular Saturday night meeting place with my friends. We rarely put skates on though. If we had any quarters we sometimes played *Pac-Man* or *Centipede* video games but we usually snuck away and did other things around town so our parents wouldn't know where we were.

Most of the time, we hung out in the woods behind the skate center. That's where a short, steep embankment lead down to the train tracks that ran through town. The hidden railway became our secret hideout where we dared each other to smoke cigarettes and drink alcohol for the first time. I never hesitated to try them. My curiosity consistently won over my weak conscience. I didn't seem to care much about getting in trouble anymore.

Another of our favorite places to hangout was the Red Geranium pizza place in town. There were always thirty or forty kids there from surrounding schools. It was a great place to go on Friday nights to meet cute boys.

One night my friends and I flirted with a group of older boys we had never seen before. They asked if we wanted to go out drinking with them, so we agreed. It felt great to be noticed by college-aged guys, since we were barely sixteen at the time.

My buddies and I climbed in their car. They took us to a dead-end road, where we parked to hold our own private party. We stood under the streetlights and drank beer together while we got to know each other. One of the boys was a tough looking nineteen-year-old guy with long hair, a mustache, and a black leather jacket. He made a lot of suggestive sexual innuendos that made me blush, but it felt nice to have his attention. At one point he leaned over and tried to kiss me. This made me nervous because it was so abrupt and unexpected. I told him I was uncomfortable kissing him yet, because I hardly knew him. He assured me he liked me a lot and wanted to go out sometime. So I gave in when he tried again.

Later that week he called me at home and asked if I wanted to go out for ice cream. I was excited to be asked out on my first real car date. When I asked my mother for permission, she was hesitant, as usual. I suppose most parents would be reluctant to let their daughter go on their first date with a boy they don't know.

A short time later he arrived at my house and knocked on the front door. When I invited him inside to meet my mom he immediately got upset. He said, "No! I'm not coming in."

My heart sank. I said, "My mother will never let me go if you don't come in. Just say hi and we'll get out of here."

He reluctantly stepped inside, but didn't say much when

she introduced herself. His demeanor made me uncomfortable. I assumed he was just shy, or nervous, so I shrugged it off.

When we finally turned to leave Mom looked at me and shook her head with disapproval. She said she didn't want me to leave. I insisted, "You never want me to have any fun. We're just getting an ice cream cone. It's no big deal. I'll be home soon."

I defiantly walked outside and got into his rusty old brown El Camino.

On our way into town, he drove right past the ice cream parlor we were supposed to go to. I assumed he just missed the turn, so I inquired. He said he had a big surprise for me first and kept driving.

A few minutes later we pulled up to a small house in a part of town I wasn't familiar with. He said, "Come on in. I need to take care of something for my mother real quick; then we'll go."

I followed him inside. He walked straight to a bedroom that had motorcycle posters hanging all over the walls. He sat on the edge of the bed, then grabbed my hand and pulled me towards him. Then he attempted to kiss me.

I was anxious about being in the small house alone so I pulled away and said, "I really think we should go."

He grabbed me again, but this time he used more force to push my body onto the bed. He immediately started unbuttoning my shirt and pulling down my pants. I couldn't believe what was happening. I sat up and said, "No, I'm not ready for this. I don't want to!"

He shoved me back down and straddled me with his heavy body so I couldn't move. Then he grabbed both of my arms and held them together over my head with the strength of his left arm and upper body, while he finished removing my pants with the other. I was terrified and had no idea what to do.

Once he positioned me as he wanted, he pushed his own pants down. My heart raced completely out of control. I was overcome with nausea and wanted to throw up. I tried to twist my body and free my arms from his restraint, but he was too strong. Then, without warning, he pushed himself into me with a quick and violent thrust.

I writhed in pain. I bit my lower lip and tears filled my eyes while I tried to endure the agonizing torture.

While he had his way with me, I noticed another motorcycle poster hanging on the ceiling above the bed. I became entranced with the picture and imagined riding away on the bike into the mountainous scenery it was photographed in. I used my powerful imagination as a way to escape the situation I was actually in.

A few minutes later he released my arms and rolled off of me. I was relieved that the suffering was finally over. When I sat up to get dressed, I noticed blood all over his bed. It confused me because I knew it wasn't my period. I was afraid I had been seriously hurt. I immediately grabbed my pants and pulled them on as quickly as possible. When he saw the stains, he abruptly yelled at me, "You virgin!"

He continued yelling at me while he gathered the sheets from the bed and put them into a washing machine in the next room. He was furious about the mess. My anxiety grew. I was speechless, almost comatose. He told me to get in the car so he could take me home. I thought about running but I wasn't familiar with the surrounding area. I didn't even know which direction to go to find a pay phone. Plus, I really didn't want my mother to find out about what happened, so I quietly obeyed and got in his car.

I didn't say one word to him on the drive home. However, he continued to mock my virginity. He made it very clear what a disappointment I had been to him.

As we passed the ice cream store on the way home, I suddenly felt all my hopes and dreams of a beautiful marriage one day literally fly out the window. I thought, *Nobody can love me now. I'm ruined.*

When we pulled into my driveway, I quietly got out of his car and walked inside. My body was so numb I could barely feel my feet on the floor. Mom asked how my date went but all I could say was, "It was no big deal."

I went straight to my bedroom, closed the door, and took off my disgusting underwear so I could hide them in the trash. For several hours I stared at my bedroom walls in a zombie-like trance, unable to even cry.

I didn't tell anybody the details of what happened for many years. I was too humiliated and assumed it was my fault. I was angry with myself for not avoiding the situation or finding a way to fight back. I was sick and tired of being taken advantage of and vowed to never trust another person. It would only be a matter of time before the dark secret I buried inside would finally rear its ugly head.

In an effort to take the edge off my chronic pain, I began drinking more than ever. It wasn't long before my love of the bottle led to a curiosity about drugs. Once that curiosity invaded my thought life I developed an intense desire to try them long before the opportunity ever presented itself. When it finally did, I was all in.

My first experience getting high was with Tricia. She scored some marijuana on a trip she took to Chicago and smuggled it home in a plastic film canister for us to try together for our first time. Because she had scored the goods, I was delegated to buy the rolling papers needed to smoke the crumbled up plant leaves.

We drove to a gas station about thirty minutes outside of town. There was less chance of being seen by someone we knew there, while I made the devious purchase. I walked inside a small dingy market, extremely nervous about my task. Cigarette papers were kept behind the counter, so I feared the man at the register would doubt my intentions and call the police. My insatiable curiosity strong-armed fear, once again, and I carried through with the plan.

The store clerk didn't even flinch at my request. He passed me the papers, took my money, and it was over in an instant. I was elated that it had been so easy! I jumped back in the car, very eager to begin my new experience.

Tricia and I drove around country back roads for a couple of hours while we toked together on a fat hog leg joint I haphazardly rolled. As I inhaled my very first puff of weed, the chaotic world that harassed me on a daily basis instantly melted away. I was immediately relaxed. Every worry, anxious thought, and physical discomfort disappeared completely. Stress and tension evaporated into a beautiful, peaceful euphoria.

Alcohol created an I-don't-care attitude that made all my cares disappear, but getting high consumed me in a different way. It was cozy and mellow instead. I was no longer assaulted by the overwhelming sensations of the world, but rather drawn into them. When I turned on the radio my soul felt like it was in communion with the music, not just listening to it. I was floating weightless and unconfined to my body, as if I was soaring through the heavens.

Using marijuana and alcohol became my primary goals for after-school outings and weekends. This required more cash flow than the occasional babysitting job was able to provide. As soon as I turned sixteen, I put in an application at the local grocery store and got my first real job. Two weeks later, after receiving my first paycheck, it was time to celebrate.

The wad of dollars was more than I'd ever had in my possession. It burned a hole straight through my pocket. I splurged with friends and bought large bottles of liquor, instead of the cheap watered down beer we usually drank. Most of my friends enjoyed drinking wine coolers but I preferred the strong, warm shock of swigging whiskey or rum.

Getting alcohol was never much of a problem for us. We visited every gas station and liquor store around town and learned quickly who carded underage buyers and who didn't. Oftentimes there was a keg party somewhere, which we had no problems crashing. If we wanted to get into a bar in Nashville that had a bouncer out front checking IDs, then we simply slipped in through the back door and snuck through the kitchen past employees. The mixture of an adrenalin rush paired with alcohol created a very enjoyable experience that I was immediately addicted to.

Hard work was required to provide enough cash for the amount of partying I wanted to do. My daily shifts were long grueling hours spent stuffing grocery bags, mopping floors, and doing price checks. It was quite monotonous at times, so I found creative ways to make the job a lot more fun. For example, I made up a game called Buggy Joust with coworkers. Each person stood on one end of a cart and then rolled towards each other as fast as we could in the parking lot, only swerving at the last second if we didn't want to crash. It was a spinoff of the classic game Chicken.

Other times we raced carts up and down rows of cars to see who could go the fastest. If we accidentally slammed into vehicles or left scratches and dents on the customer's cars, we quickly walked back inside the store as if nothing happened.

We also had manager-approved competitions to see who could pack the most bags in the shortest amount of time. The store supervisors recognized my efficient packing abilities and always asked me to assist if someone famous came into the store like Minnie Pearl, Roseanne Cash, Amy Grant, and Tom T. Hall.

My desire to earn enough cash to purchase weed and alcohol began to compete with my desire to be out consuming the weed and alcohol. So it wasn't long before the lines between work and play became blurred. I no longer waited to clock out before consuming. In fact, I found ways to get high on the job instead.

Sometimes my fifteen minute breaks were spent with friends driving around the block to smoke a joint. However, it was much more exciting to sneak into the cold meat locker in the back of the grocery store and take a few hits there. That added a shot of adrenalin as well! I also kept a thermos of gin or vodka in the employee break room, where I could easily walk by and take a few gulps in between helping customers. Interestingly, everyone praised my pleasant, outgoing personality at work. In my addicted mind, this seemed to be a good rationalization to continue my illegal consumption; it was helping me come out of my shell.

By the time I reached my junior year in high school, I had figured out ways to indulge at school as well. Drinking and smoking pot became a daily habit. Each morning I purchased a container of orange juice in the school cafeteria then poured vodka or gin into the carton. I sipped on it during class and nobody had a clue.

In art class there was a separate attached room in the back that had a ventilator and fan, where students would spray their charcoal drawings with fixative. I often took a quick hit or two off a joint there while finishing my projects. A few students caught on to what I was doing, but none of my teachers ever found out. Although it did come extremely close one time.

One day Tricia and I went behind the school to take a cigarette break and get high between classes. We went to an area where students weren't supposed to go, but thought we'd get away with it. Just as I held a joint between my lips and started to flick my lighter, the doors flew open behind us. The assistant principal, Mr. Williams, walked out like an old western sheriff pushing his way through saloon doors.

I quickly tucked the joint into my fist while he questioned what we were doing. Tricia told him we just needed a private place to talk because she was having a bad day. Then he noticed the cigarette she was holding. It was legal to smoke at sixteen back then, and we were even allowed to smoke at our school, but only in the designated smoking courtyard. Behind the school was not a designated area. He shot me a suspicious look and firmly told both of us follow him to the principal's office.

As we walked behind Mr. Williams on our way to

certain punishment, I looked at Tricia and she soundlessly mouthed the words, "Drop the joint." I shook my head in disagreement. Weed was like gold to me, so I wasn't about to get rid of it. I stuffed it inside my bra instead.

When we got inside the office, Mr. Williams told the principal, whom students referred to as JP, where we had been found smoking. JP asked Tricia for her purse; then dumped the contents on his desk. Tricia complained, "What do you think you're doing? That's my private property!"

He said, "You better hope all I find in here are cigarettes."

My heart sank. I knew I was about to get busted. As I sat on the edge of my seat in a chair against the wall, I suddenly became aware that the joint was barely hanging inside my bra. It was literally about to drop through my shirt at any second. That's because I always fastened my bra loosely, since I hated how it felt to wear one.

Suddenly JP stated, "I'm calling Mrs. Pierson in here to search you two." His threat seemed to indicate he was calling for a strip search by having the female teacher come in.

As I scrambled for ways to discard the illegal substance from my undergarments, Tricia immediately spoke up and demanded our rights. She fussed, "What you are doing is inappropriate. You better let us go or I'm going to contact my parent's lawyer. You will not get away with this!"

I was certain her attitude would only get us in more trouble, but it actually worked. Her brave confidence made him back down, and he actually let us go.

As soon as we were safely away in the hall, I pulled the joint out from underneath my shirt and laughed. I said, "Should we try again?" Tricia didn't think it was funny.

On homecoming day, I pushed the boundaries even further by bringing a large igloo cooler full of lemonade mixed with gin to school. I hid it in the girls' bathroom by putting the jug of happy juice on top of the far corner toilet. Then I locked the stall door and crawled underneath the door to keep our stash hidden. Throughout the day, whenever I wanted to indulge, I just crawled back in when nobody was looking and gulped some down.

That afternoon we had a big homecoming parade. Students drove their painted cars and flower-decorated floats through town to rally people together for our big football game that night. My friends and I met in the bathroom beforehand to make sure the festivities would be even more fun. We drank until we had a sufficient buzz then went outside and got in line for the parade with the other students and teachers.

Instead of riding on a float or in a car, like everybody else, my friends and I had a unique form of transportation. It was a tiny Japanese motorcycle called a Motocompo, which Tricia owned. However, it looked nothing like a regular motorcycle. It was a third of the size and shaped like a long yellow rectangle sitting on tiny wheels. It was so compact that the handlebars and seat folded inside the body so it could fit inside the trunk of a car. It was really cute and nobody else in town had one. It always drew special attention to us when people saw us riding it.

Somehow Tricia, Karen, and I squeezed our three skinny little bodies onto the bike together. We rode all through town laughing and singing as loudly as we could the whole way. We had a blast as we whizzed by and drove circles around parade onlookers in our inebriated state. As dangerous as it was, I wanted the moment of fun and the feeling of freedom to last forever.

Whenever periods of drunkenness or euphoria wore off, the warnings I heard in church and school echoed through my mind.

You're being foolish. You're gonna get caught. You're gonna die. You're going to hell.

Sometimes I got paranoid that something bad would happen if I continued abusing substances as much I was. However, I rationalized my bad habits because of the comfort they brought me. The seeming benefits greatly outweighed trying to exist without them. Against my own better judgment, I decided to use whatever I could, any time I got the chance. I just needed to increase my chances.

My friends and I frequented parties around town with other kids who liked to party. Johnny was one of those people. He was a senior football player at our school. He was usually the life of the party because of his crazy sense of humor and outgoing personality. I thought he was adorable and immediately took a liking to him. A few days after we met, he asked me out. I was blown away that someone so popular and outgoing was interested in me.

On our first date, as soon as we pulled out of my driveway, Johnny handed me a pipe full of marijuana and asked if I wanted a hit. A giant smirk grew across my face. I was all for it. We were high before we even left my neighborhood. I thought, "This guy really knows how to take care of me!" I knew I'd be spending a lot of time with him. He was sweet, charming, and always ready with my favorite intoxicating cure.

Things got serious between Johnny and me pretty quick.

In fact, he started telling me he loved me after just a few dates. And after a few short months, he even asked if I would marry him once we graduated from high school. I said yes but asked him to keep our plans a secret until we were ready to tell our parents.

Because of Johnny's profession of love for me, I gave him 100 percent of myself physically. I compromised my convictions, because I got what I wanted most too: to be loved, accepted, and understood.

Being around Johnny was always fun. He introduced me to even more friends who liked to party. We played poker and went swimming, camping, exploring caves, and on many four-wheeling excursions in the woods. Crawling over treacherous terrains was something my new friends took very seriously too. They even modified their Jeeps and trucks with giant tires, roll bars, and better suspensions to overcome landscapes that a normal 4x4 couldn't even tackle. We had some true southern redneck fun.

Each weekend became a new challenge for us to go where no man had gone before. Our muddy caravans climbed rocky hills, forged slippery streams, and plowed through thick brush until we found secluded fields. There we held our own private parties and listened to bands like Led Zeppelin and The Rolling Stones as we melted into the music in our drug-induced euphoria.

Sometimes our excursions took us to secret places where my friends had marijuana plants growing, so we could check on their growth. Other times we drove to remote cliffs where we took turns rappelling down the jagged, 100-foot walls. No matter what we did, I always felt safe and secure with the rowdy, adventurous bunch. Besides, they had police scanners that warned if cops were alerted to our whereabouts. We always got away in plenty of time whenever they came looking for us.

My parents were ignorant to my problems during the first several years of substance abuse. However, the more frequently I used, the more agitated I became when I wasn't. Eventually the friction between us grew more intense. I hated being at home, sober, with nothing to do but feel guilty for the reckless path my life was headed down. I knew it would hurt my parents if they ever found out, but I didn't know any other way to cope with the pain and secrets I had buried inside.

Grief over my life tortured me. However, I continued to justify bad decisions with my irrational, dysfunctional thinking. My attempts to do the right thing were often misunderstood or completely unnoticed by everyone. It was much easier to medicate symptoms of anxiety, depression, and physical discomfort. I found peace there; if only for a while.

CHAPTER ELEVEN

Shrinks and Mentors

FIRST LADY NANCY REAGAN encouraged us in her 1980s advertising campaign to "Just Say No" to illegal drugs. She warned of the dangers and pitfalls that recreational drug use could lead to. I mocked her words of wisdom by writing, "Just Say No to Nancy" on my jeans with paint. What I didn't want to admit, though, was that she was right. It didn't take long before my drug experimentation turned into bigger problems.

The chronic stress from the overwhelming assault on my senses, as well as the deep-seated anguish I kept buried inside, were unbearable to deal with if I wasn't high. It was the only thing I found that provided any relief. However, masking my hurt and anger just allowed it to fester in darkness. Sober moments became even more desperate and painful. Anger began to erupt into increasing outbursts of violent rage.

Fighting with my parents was nothing new. It had been a daily routine since the moment I was born. Our relationship was strained, at best. Unfortunately, the monster who grew beneath the surface eventually became uncontrollable and reared its ugly head in truly despicable ways.

Arguments with my mom continuously escalated with each fight being worse than the one before. Infuriated by her attempts to rescue me by preaching about Jesus, I often responded by screaming how much I hated her. Anything to make her stop. I even pushed her away with curled up fists if she got too close. I just wanted her to stop trying so hard to change me. She couldn't possibly understand how much pain I was really in. I was convinced if she knew the truth about all the insidious things I had done she would realize that Jesus couldn't help either.

One afternoon her gospel presentation drove me completely over the edge. Through a heated exchange of words, I left the house in a fury. Despite her pleas and tears, her message made me feel more alienated than cared for. She was brokenhearted and desperate for a way to connect with me. She was completely unaware of why my personal struggle was so intense, but I couldn't bring myself to tell her. I was too embarrassed.

Reckless and without abandon, I tore down the driveway in my small car. I found an old gravel road where I could be alone and let off steam. As my little car sped around each corner of the unpaved surface, dust and rocks filled the sky behind me.

You are a disappointment to everyone. You are worthless. Useless. No good!

Flying into a straightaway, I pulled the handbrake and jerked the steering wheel as hard as I could. The car spun violently around in the dirt. It was a physical manifestation of the swirling rage inside my heart. I felt desperate and tired of wrestling for peace.

Screaming at the top of my lungs, I questioned God, "What's wrong with me? Why do bad things keep happening? Why can't anybody understand?"

Foolishly weaving back and forth down both sides of the road, I sped around like a raving lunatic. Then, almost as if another person were sitting in the passenger seat beside me, the same voice that tormented me with name-calling began to encourage me with a way out of my pain.

Drive into that big tree over there. Get it over with! You don't deserve this life. Nobody understands. Take control. Make the pain stop.

I stomped on the gas pedal and pressed it to the floor. The tires spun on the road underneath until they gained traction again. I headed directly towards a fat tree that was just off the edge of the road about a hundred feet in front of me.

Enough is enough. You can do it! Go! Go! Go!

At the last possible second, without even thinking, I slammed on the brakes. Barely maintaining control of the vehicle, I managed to navigate out of the path of certain destruction. My car slid sideways as it bounced over the rough terrain full of ruts, rocks, limbs, and overgrown brush. A much smaller tree eventually stopped my car in its tracks. The shocking brutal force of the impact scared me. Fortunately, I wasn't hurt. The tree I hit was a twig in comparison to what I had originally aimed for. I knew I had almost hurt or destroyed myself.

Bawling like a newborn infant who had just been thrust into a confusing and overwhelming world, I gasped for air through the flood of tears.

"God? Are you up there? Can you hear me? If you're so real, why do you let bad things happen to me? Why don't you care about me? Oh, I get it. You must be angry with me too! I'm just an impure, disappointing, no-good whore!"

I beat my hands on the steering wheel with all my might until the negative energy inside my body was completely depleted. I finally slumped over like a useless bag of bones. I cried for what seemed like hours, until I was numb with exhaustion.

I eventually got my car back onto the dirt road, but it wasn't an easy task. Fortunately there was no major damage done due to a thick front bumper and good brakes. I didn't really want to die, but I couldn't bear for things to remain the way they were either.

Drugs and alcohol successfully sedated my discomfort for short periods of time, but life only seemed to get dramatically worse overall. Rather than expose any dark secrets, I built a thick, tough exterior to protect my gaping, sensitive wounds. With gnashed teeth and clinched fists, I motivated myself to try harder to survive—by any means possible.

The more frequent my drug use and drinking became the less vigilant and overprotective I became of hiding my habits. Eventually my parents discovered the truth. My mother describes that day as being as painful as if someone told her I died. Shock and grief literally took the wind out of her. She was devastated. From my perspective, my parent's discovery was too late to do anything about it. Smoking and drinking had been cemented into my lifestyle for several years by then, so their warnings and concerns couldn't persuade me to stop. Besides, I wasn't about to trade what little peace and comfort drugs gave me for their peace of mind.

My mother responded to my drug use the same way any desperate mother would who wanted to save their child from certain destruction. She relentlessly pursued anybody who could intervene and help. She started with my Sunday school teacher, Allyson.

Allyson was a jovial character who was easy to be around because of her friendly, optimistic spirit. She led the small group of high school girls at my southern Baptist church where I had been dragged every Sunday morning for years. My mother rallied her support, hoping the relationship she developed with me would help her break through.

Allyson started driving by my house and job at random times, in an effort to talk with me. Her seemingly sudden concern was alarming and made me paranoid. I finally agreed to meet her one afternoon at a field near my house, hoping a short discussion would appease her.

Allyson tried her best to dig deeper into why I acted out. She asked if I drank to fit in with other kids at school. I admitted that social drinking wasn't my motive. I drank to get drunk. When she asked how often I got drunk my response was, "Every day."

I could see the concern in Allyson's eyes while she tried to uncover the source of my escapism, but my walls were too thick to penetrate. I didn't want to be rescued. I wanted to be left alone. The fact that someone finally cared about *why* I was hurting was nice but I saw no benefit in uncovering the truth. The vices used to keep my demons hidden seemed to suffice for the time being so I kept Allyson at arm's length. I refused to accept her appeals that Jesus Christ could change my life.

She wouldn't be saying these things if she knew everything about me. This is total nonsense. Jesus wouldn't want to forgive someone as screwed up as me.

Despite my rejection of Allyson at that time, my mother didn't stop pursuing other ways to help. In fact, one afternoon she picked me up from school early for a doctor's appointment. I assumed it was time for my annual physical to validate my health for participating in school sports. However, when the nurse called me to the back room, the doctor who met me was wearing a suit and tie rather than the typical white lab coat.

The strange doctor sat next to a large desk in a room full of books. It wasn't the usual cold white room with cotton swabs and a paper covered table. Instead of a tongue depressor, he held a clipboard.

He asked a lot of personal questions that made me uncomfortable. I finally realized he was a shrink. I felt shammed and violated by the surprise interrogation, so I declined to answer. Instead, the doctor received an earful of concerns I had for my mother, who I argued was having a nervous breakdown.

During my attempt to deflect his concerns onto my mom, he scribbled a lot of notes on his formal pad of paper, which made me even more paranoid. As soon as the appointment was over, a slew of curse words blasted from my lips towards my mom for tricking me into a psychologist's office without my approval. However, that didn't stop her from trying again.

A couple of months later she *said* I had a dental appointment, but I knew better. I went along with her conniving ploy because I hoped to convince the doctor she was a raving psychopath because of her chronic deceit and manipulation. However, when we got into the office I was the one surprised again.

Mommy dearest pulled a handful of my drawings from her purse and handed them to the doctor. He carefully studied each one as he scribbled more notes in my file. Furious, I yelled, "How did you find my artwork? Have you been going through my stuff? How dare you invade my privacy!"

My illustrations had evolved over time from silly cartoons, animal portraits, and landscapes into twisted and disturbing scenes. One of the drawings the doctor reviewed depicted an emaciated, elderly woman with no clothes on. Her face was anguished with fear as she descended a steep staircase into hell, where demonic hands reached up to welcome her home.

Another drawing was the close-up of a screaming man's face, with deep worried wrinkles. He struggled to loosen a hangman's noose that was tied around his neck.

A third drawing portrayed another naked human trapped inside a small transparent cube that was barely big enough to house his body. He was curled in the fetal position with hands and feet pressed against the glass. He looked desperate to push his way out of the claustrophobic chamber of horror.

Most of my drawings were sketches mindlessly drawn while listening to lectures in chemistry or history class. I hadn't meant for them to be seen by anybody. Regardless, Mom felt it was important for the doctor to know exactly how disturbed I really was.

Fury whirled inside me again. Not only for being taken to another psychologist, but because they mocked my artwork by saying it allowed them insights into how I felt. Their judgment felt like betrayal and ridicule. There was no way they could know how I was thinking or feeling.

My high school principal and guidance counselors also got involved with the many intervention attempts. Once my mother clued them in to my problems they investigated my attendance patterns at school. That's when they discovered I had skipped three months of study hall. Otherwise I maintained good grades. However, since I had been delinquent from the boring, unproductive non-class since the semester began, they chose to discipline me with Saturday morning detentions.

For several weekends in a row, I had to clean up the school's parking lot, football fields, and bathrooms. I was left alone as I walked around the campus for hours and picked up trash. Naturally, I completed the chore after getting high on the vacant football field. Oddly enough, I enjoyed my punishment. The time alone was reinvigorating and peaceful.

After numerous failed intervention attempts from family, church friends, counselors, and school leaders, our local law enforcement team was next. My run-in with them wasn't one that my mom coordinated though. Rather, my time spent with them was a result of my own stupidity.

I was drinking in a public park with friends in the middle of the night when a police officer busted us. Since I was the one underage and out past curfew, I was sentenced to a full day at the courthouse with other rebellious kids so the cops could attempt to scare us straight.

For eight long hours one Saturday, I was surrounded by cops in the cold courthouse in downtown Nashville. They showed violent videos of death and destruction to warn me what alcohol and drugs could do. It was also mandatory to write an essay about the sins I had committed and a letter of apology to my parents. After reading my notes to the judge at the end of the day, he gave me a stern warning. He was convinced I was going to end up in prison one day if I didn't shape up. Unfortunately, his intimidating words just fueled my animosity towards people even more. I was tired of being told I was on the road to nowhere.

Why doesn't anybody believe in me?

I can't blame my parents for wanting to help me get off the reckless path my life was on. They would have done anything to save me. But from my warped perspective at the time, I felt violated, assaulted, and unworthy. My problems felt bigger than anything they, or anybody else, could help me with. I figured if time really healed all wounds, then keeping myself distracted from the pain for a while was all I really needed.

Boy was that assumption wrong.

CHAPTER TWELVE

Combat for Control

———————◆———————

HIGH SCHOOL STARTED with a whimper and went out with a bang. Somehow my friends and I miraculously survived four long, crazy years studying together, crying with each other, and laughing until we peed our pants. We witnessed each other's first loves and losses, near misses with law enforcement, and trouble with parents. When graduation night finally arrived, we celebrated more than just our educational achievements; we celebrated our lasting friendship.

The girls that made up my innermost circle of friends bought matching outfits for our graduation party. We wore colorful Bermuda shorts, Converse tennis shoes, and identical shirts that had "Buddy System" written across the front. We proudly declared that we had made it through high school together: one for all and all for one! We partied all night long as we sang and danced alongside the rest of the class of 1986.

At the end of our graduation celebration, the Buddy

System made pinky promises as we stood in a circle together. We swore to remain friends for the rest of our lives, no matter what distances or challenges came between us.

The commitment from my friends, and my continued relationship with my boyfriend Johnny, gave me a renewed assurance and confidence that I could handle whatever life threw at me—good or bad. Being loved and accepted as I was brought a lot of strength to press on. It gave me confidence to face the world, as opposed to hiding in my fragile shell. As long as I had them, I knew I would be okay. Most of us were planning to attend the same college together so the future looked bright.

A few short weeks after graduation, the moment I looked forward to for many years finally arrived. I flew from my parent's nest and into a small dorm room at Middle Tennessee State University. It also happened to be my eighteenth birthday. My parents didn't share my enthusiasm for the big day though. They feared my substance abuse would spiral even more out of control. I assumed that independence was exactly what I needed to gain more control over my life, but you know what they say about assuming.

I enrolled as an art major. Most of my classes were held in an old farmhouse that was remodeled on the inside to create rooms for painting and drawing. This creative space was affectionately called the Art Barn. My professors taught much more than art history and various methods of design though. They expanded my mind with their personal rants on philosophy and religion. Their insights were usually in opposition to the worldview I'd been exposed to in my childhood. Therefore, I wrestled to discern what I really believed for myself.

I loved being around other creative students. It was fun to watch my artistic style emerge and differentiate from theirs. The only class I wasn't too fond of was figure drawing. Sketching nude models made me extremely uncomfortable, especially because we had to sketch an overweight, middle-aged Sasquatch of a man. I didn't enjoy being required to pay attention to the specific details required to duplicate his image on paper with charcoal, if you know what I mean. You can't unsee that! His hairy, unkempt, blubbery image was etched into my brain forever. Otherwise, I felt unhindered from expressing myself freely. I esteemed this feeling of creative freedom as success.

On afternoons my friends and I didn't have class we often drove to a swimming hole we found near campus. Another option was to climb up to the roof of our dorm and relax while lying in the sun. At night the same rooftop provided a great vantage point on campus to people watch and stargaze. And of course, get high.

As college freshmen, we attended numerous parties held at fraternity houses around campus; ID was never required. We indulged in as much beer as we could consume from their free-running kegs. Being inside such crowded places, where people yelled at one another over the loud music, always led me into a frenzied sensory overload which intensified the effects of alcohol for me. I often got sick but refused to be a party pooper so I endured the torture just to try and fit in.

By far my favorite place to hang out was a secluded area my friends and I discovered on top of one of the tallest hills near Murfreesboro. A dirt path twisted through the woods to the top of the hill, far away from the bustling city life below. At the summit an old fire tower had been erected, where watchmen searched for wildfires in the surrounding wilderness in years past.

The elevated metal structure stood about eighty feet tall, and hovered high above the tallest trees in the woods it protruded from. A small staircase zigzagged up through the center of the structure to a tiny square room at the very top. However, because the tower was no longer in use, the stairs that went from ground to the first level were no longer there. They were probably removed to prevent people from climbing. That didn't stop us though.

The first horizontal beam was about ten feet off the ground. It required a boost by friends to reach it. Other times I parked my car at the base and used the hood as a stepping stool. Then my friends and I hoisted ourselves up to begin our ascent.

We scaled the outer beams like Spiderman, and cautiously maneuvered our way towards the stairs. Hanging like primates from ginormous monkey bars, our feet dangled high above the earth as we shimmied our way across the structure. It required strength, agility, and balance to make it up safely. It wasn't an easy climb, but well worth the effort when we made it.

Arriving at the top after a nerve-racking feat rewarded us with a view that was absolutely remarkable. We shared joints and laughs together as we floated in the clouds in our private backwoods skyscraper. It was truly awesome.

The fire tower challenge was exhilarating and fun. I admit there were many times I was afraid we wouldn't make it to the ground alive. Obviously intoxicated, we fumbled our way down the metal mountain on numerous occasions. Somehow we always managed to find the bottom without falling, and the death-defying stunt satiated my adrenalin-junkie bones.

Saturdays at our suitcase college were typically desolate because most students went home on the weekends. My friends and I usually stayed together and searched for parties. However, because the frat houses and dorms were mostly abandoned, we often took road trips to other cities to find some action.

Tricia, Wendy, and I usually packed into Karen's tiny blue Yugo like circus clowns and set off for our wild adventure. After purchasing a sack full of Krystals to eat along the way, we would head towards a different college town in search of a good time. Speeding down the highway, we sang along with the Violent Femmes and The B-52s at the top of our lungs. We didn't have a care in the world. Our fun-filled trips led us to numerous football games, clubs, and fraternities at the University of Tennessee and Ole Miss. We took full advantage of our freedom to explore the world and I loved every single minute!

Being able to do whatever I wanted, whenever I wanted, gave me a sense of security and control over my life that I embraced with open arms. However, the more freedom I gained, the more I resisted any new boundaries or restrictions that came along. Dorm living, for one, had its ups and downs. Boys weren't allowed inside our rooms, so I saw the restriction as a personal challenge I needed to overcome.

A large security desk sat in the lobby where guards checked each person that went in and out of our building. Bright lights covered the sidewalks around the dorm at night. I devised a plan to sneak Johnny and his friends in past the gauntlet and into the back fire escape stairwell, just for the simple thrill of getting away with it.

My friends and I stood at different lookout points around our dorm and ushered the boys in one by one as the coast became clear from guards and other students. They made it to our rooms unseen where we partied together for several hours. We did this numerous times.

Unfortunately, one night, when it was time for the guys to leave, the guard on duty saw them exiting the back door. Security yelled for them to stop, but they ran as fast as they could to their get-away car which was parked nearby. My friends and I scrambled back to our rooms, hoping we wouldn't be identified as their accomplices. Luckily, their car peeled away right as the guard got to them, and none of us were ever caught.

We also weren't allowed to have alcohol in the campus dorms, but I kept a stash hidden in my closet. My secret treasure included an assortment of hard liquors like vodka, whiskey, and rum. One night, on a whim to simply add to my collection, I bought some tequila. After successfully getting the bottle to my room, I foolishly bet my friends I could drink thirteen shots and still be okay. I honestly have no idea why I made such a ridiculous claim, other than thirteen was my favorite number, and I thought I could handle my liquor. Mind you, this reasoning was nothing short of stupid.

As I downed each shot I repeated, "Give me another." Against the better advice of my friends, I persisted with the self-imposed challenge until all thirteen shots were down. I didn't feel their full effects at first and proudly proclaimed my success. Shortly afterwards, my friends and I skipped across campus to the student cinema to watch the *Rocky Horror Picture Show*.

As I sat in the small theatre and watched costumed characters fill the seats around me, I began to feel dizzy. The room went on full spin cycle as soon as the overhead lights turned off and the big screen lit up. At first, I joyfully sang along with the others to the opening credits of the science fiction musical. Then things suddenly took a turn for the worse.

The music, laughter, and boisterous caroling blended into a frenzied nonsensical mess. My vision blurred and eyes crossed with delirium. Gut-wrenching nausea violently blindsided me. I didn't even pause to inform my friends I was feeling sick. I simply took off running and hoped to make it somewhere safe to throw up. My dorm was only about a hundred yards away so I headed in that direction as fast as I could go and prayed I would make it.

About half-way home the alcohol inside gurgled to the point I couldn't contain it any longer. I puked behind a bush with rocket-launching propulsion. Unfortunately, this didn't bring any relief. My head swirled so fast I could no longer stand. However, I didn't want to stay on the sidewalk and risk exposing my deplorable condition to whomever walked by. So, I crawled on my knees the rest of the way back to my dorm room. Slowly.

Once I got to my building I avoided the busy elevators and snuck up the back stairwell. In my stupor, I had to physically wrestle myself up each stair to the fifth floor. Before I could find comfort in my bed, my stomach started convulsing again. I crawled, or more like slithered, across the cold tile floor to the bathroom. That's where I spent the next several hours praying to the porcelain god.

The next day I was embarrassed at how sick I had been.

My whole body suffered from the previous night's ordeal. The saddest part was that it didn't stop me from drinking too much again. In fact, I repeated the same pathetic scene numerous times that year.

Once I became a sophomore, I moved into an apartment near campus. There I wouldn't have to sneak boys or alcohol to my room. However, having more freedom didn't provide the control I sought after. In fact, my bad habits became a very serious problem. I can't recall much about that year, probably because it lacked any sober moments.

After long nights of drinking and smoking, I started taking speed to stay awake for class during the day. The excessive combinations created a very unsettling and restless feeling that made it impossible to relax or feel comfortable. Getting high and drunk wasn't fun anymore, but I felt even worse when I was sober. There was no longer a way to relieve my chronic misery. I was sick of using drugs and alcohol, but even sicker without them.

My closest relationships suffered that year as well. I desperately wanted to change my lifestyle but knew I'd continue on the same destructive path if I stayed with my boyfriend, Johnny. So, I broke up. I knew I would never stop using drugs unless I forced myself away from them. It was a noble attempt, but ultimately my decision did nothing more for me than lose a great friend.

At the same time, Tricia moved to Knoxville to finish her degree at the University of Tennessee and Karen left for cosmetology school. Wendy continued at MTSU but had a steady boyfriend she had become engaged to, so she spent all of her time with him planning their fairy tale future. Loneliness grabbed me by the throat and mocked me at a time

I needed encouragement most.

After a few depressing months, I finally met three new girls at a party who were looking for a fourth roommate, so I decided to move in with them. They were friendly and kind, but I never connected with them the same way I had with my original buddy system. I found myself feeling even lonelier. Unfortunately, I didn't gain any control over my drug and alcohol habit as planned either. In fact, my abuse continued with a vengeance. My life was desperately out of control, but no matter how hard I tried to do better, I just couldn't take a step in the right direction.

I eventually started having blackouts where large periods of time were completely erased from my memory. More and more frequently people told me about things I had done that were both humiliating and horrifying. I had no recollection of days on end.

I was angry with myself, but also scared because I knew my problem was serious. I wasn't sure where to go or how to get help. Not feeling like I had any options, I tried to convince myself that everything would be okay if I just paced myself better.

One evening my parents surprised me with a visit to my apartment to see how I was doing. It's an understatement to say it didn't go well. They found multiple large, empty liquor bottles scattered around my room. Not to mention, my degrading health and appearance almost sent my mom into cardiac arrest.

That night my parents made the agonizing decision to stop assisting me financially. They took my car away and sold it. They also warned they would no longer pay for college unless I stopped drinking and drugging and came home. I hated them in that moment. I assumed their love for me was conditional, even cruel, for making me more destitute than I already was. Moving back home to their restricting environment wasn't the help I was looking for. I refused to agree to their impossible terms of condition, so they cut me off. Completely.

Determined to earn a living, continue with school, and prove I could handle myself without any parental support, I submitted numerous job applications the next day. After scarcely getting by for several weeks, I was finally hired at a local grocery store.

My new job was about two miles away from my apartment. Granted, two miles isn't a terrible distance to travel on foot but because I was in class during the day, my work shifts usually weren't over until midnight. When I left the store, I had to drudge through unlit, shady neighborhood streets alone in the middle of the night. In those moments, I felt abandoned. I tried to bum rides from roommates and coworkers, but never had any extra cash to pitch in for gas. Not wanting to be a mooch I was usually on my own for the lonely treks home.

I eventually got a butterfly knife to carry on my long, dark commutes. While practicing a quick flick of the wrist to open and close the knife, I prayed out loud for God's divine protection as I walked. A deep-rooted resentment grew in my heart towards my parents with each step. I blamed them for putting me into such a dangerous situation. I failed to acknowledge my own personal responsibility in the matter and just assumed they didn't love me.

It wasn't long before my fear and anger turned to paranoia. Believing I was destined for bad things to happen, my eyes constantly shifted back and forth over my shoulder. I expected an oncoming attacker at any moment. After going through the same daily routine for several months, the paranoia eventually consumed my thoughts even when I was safe at home.

The more I believed nobody cared about me, the more I quit caring about myself. I felt lost and forsaken, without a friend to help me make it through each day. When a fellow classmate asked me to go bar hopping one weekend I was optimistic that things were turning around. So, I agreed to go.

That night we went to six or seven different bars around Murfreesboro, just to have a drink at each place and check out the scene. I thought it was a fun way to explore the various nightclubs and learn which establishments served my favorite drinks without requiring ID.

Around midnight we arrived at a shabby old dive on the dark side of town that I wasn't familiar with. We decided to have our last nightcap there, because it looked like the only place in town that was still open. We were a little more than tipsy when we arrived.

We ordered another round of drinks while we played a game of darts. When I enthusiastically proclaimed to the room that I had won the game, an older man sitting at the bar asked if he could buy me another drink. I wasn't about to refuse free alcohol. After accepting the offer and making chitchat with the stranger, he asked if I wanted to get high with him. Excited to have someone indulge me, I said yes.

As I got in the car with the man, my friend agreed to wait inside the club for me to return. We drove to a run-down neighborhood nearby where he claimed they sold some "real good stuff." We parked on the side of a dark street under a dim flickering streetlamp and waited.

A minute later two large men wearing jackets that covered their heads, approached our car. I was nervous about being in such a shady place buying drugs off the street from people I didn't know. We handed the shadowy figures a large wad of cash in exchange for a small bag. Then the two men disappeared back into the alley. I was relieved when we finally drove away.

Next the man took me to a field near the club where we could enjoy the purchase. However, when he opened the bag I realized it wasn't marijuana like I expected. Rather, it was cocaine. I knew that using another drug wasn't a wise decision. Yet, I justified trying it by convincing myself it would be okay, just this once.

He pulled a small mirror out of his glove compartment and cut the powder into lines with a razor blade on the slick surface. After removing a twenty dollar bill from his wallet, he rolled it up like a straw and handed it to me. I was growing more anxious by the moment to be reunited with my friend back at the club, but I went ahead with my turn.

As I inhaled several of the thick white trails I caught a glimpse of my reflection in the tiny mirror. I didn't enjoy seeing myself like that. I knew what I was doing was against my better judgment. So I just closed my eyes and proceeded anyway.

Within seconds I felt a sudden, but powerful, relief from my anxiety. The dizziness from alcohol even dissipated. I felt vibrantly aware with an intense clarity that sharpened my thoughts. I felt invincible, like Superman!

As I enjoyed the new vivid sensations, the man reached around my head and pulled me towards him for a kiss. I was caught off guard, and certainly not interested. My cocaine-influenced mind vigilantly presented me with numerous plans of escape. I gently pulled away with a flirtatious grin and told him I needed to go back to the bar first. That way I could let my friend know where I was so she wouldn't worry. I figured if I kept my cool and pretended to be interested in him, then I could get away. Getting upset or trying to push him away would only lead to more trouble. I had already learned that the hard way years ago.

Fortunately, he started driving back towards the club. I could tell he thought he was going to get lucky too. When we arrived, the club had been closed and nobody was there, including my friend. I had to think fast for a new way out. I knew what the man's intentions were. I couldn't waste a single minute getting away or things were going to turn bad.

Without hesitation, I immediately threw the car door open, jumped out, and ran across the road to a dimly lit gas station. I went straight to the pay phone hanging by the front door and tried to call my friend.

The man watched me for several minutes from his car. This intensified my anxiety that he was about to come after me. I yelled at him from across the street and said, "My friends are on their way to pick me up!" It wasn't true, but I hoped he would believe me. I pretended to talk on the phone for several anxious minutes.

Please go away. Please go away. God, keep me safe. Please. I don't want that man to hurt me.

Finally, he drove away.

The phone rang and rang for several minutes but my friend never answered. I panicked. It was three thirty in the morning. I had no idea where I was or which direction to go.

On top of that, there was a strange man high on cocaine that was probably sitting somewhere nearby watching me. I cursed myself for getting into the horrible situation. I fervently appealed to God to keep me safe as I strolled out into the darkness again.

I wandered up and down abandoned roads and alleys, looking for anything that seemed familiar. I needed a clue for which way to go. Somehow, after stumbling around the shadowy streets for a couple of hours, I managed to find my friend's house. I couldn't believe I made it safely without further incident. The situation seemed to parallel my inner journey of wandering aimlessly through life.

The more I fought for control over my life, the worse I made it. I knew I was on a path of destruction. I was destitute, afraid, and desperately lonely. I was doing things I didn't even want to do. Regardless, I was determined to prove to the world that I couldn't be beaten down; no matter how hard it came against me.

My desire to overcome challenges and do something good with myself was losing the life-or-death combat with drugs. Freedom and independence from parents hadn't provided the peace I was looking for. Unfortunately, surrender just wasn't an option I was willing to entertain. Instead, the war raged on.

CHAPTER THIRTEEN

Illuminating the Shadow World

***

GROWING UP, my parents, counselors, and Sunday school teachers consistently presented a Christian worldview to me, so I never doubted God's existence. However, I found it impossible to comply with His unreasonable rules and restrictions. I struggled to surrender my allegiance to Him because I assumed that all my negative experiences were a direct result of His wrath. I truly believed He was disappointed in me, so I wanted to hide.

Occasionally, in church, I heard that God wanted a relationship with me. However, I couldn't reconcile that with my personal life experiences. God demanded purity and holiness, which I had lost very early in life. I felt unlovable, ashamed and even disgusting. While I believed He was there, I felt unworthy of His communion. Like everybody else who tried to get close to me, I kept God at arm's length.

Even so, I still believed there was an active spiritual world around me—an invisible dimension which included both angels and demons. My curiosity for how life intersected with the unseen grew even stronger as my life spiraled out of control. My new college roommates also shared my belief about supernatural beings. Although they were more interested in studying witchcraft, and experimenting with black magic, than having anything to do with the Bible.

Seeking guidance from the spirit world was something they took very seriously. They claimed the dark arts gave them courage and direction, which I needed. Desperate for relief from my insecurities, I decided to participate in various occultist activities with them. Looking to the dark side for help felt like a good idea because my sins wouldn't be under constant scrutiny from their god.

My three roommates often used their Ouija board to ask the spirit world questions about the afterlife. On several occasions I played along with their attempts to conjure a spirit; assuming it was just an innocent game.

One night the four of us sat on the floor circled around the game together. A single candle flickered in the darkness to illuminate the board. We gently placed our fingertips on the triangle pointer used to navigate the various letters and words to start the game. One of my roommates, who claimed to be a practicing Wiccan, began asking questions out loud.

With each outspoken inquiry, the triangle moved slowly beneath our hands in response. It stopped on each letter we needed to remember. I doubted the sincerity of the ritual and accused my roommates of messing with me when the first few words came together. However, they insisted they hadn't forced or directed the movements in any way.

My roommate made further appeals to the spirit realm, specifically for a lost and hurting soul to speak with us. I continued to scoff. Then, without warning, our fingers began to move rapidly across the black letters at a furious pace. The board spelled out a stream of interesting answers while my heart pounded with anxiety. The energized room was charged full of static electricity that made the hair on my arms stand straight up in the air like thorns.

When my roommate asked who was communicating with us, the board spelled T-H-O-M-A-S. When asked to share more details about who Thomas was, it spelled V-I-C-A-R. None of us knew what a vicar was so I found a dictionary on the bookshelf behind us. The definition read, "A person acting as a priest or a member of the clergy who is in charge of a church." Our fascination grew more intense. We spent the next hour interrogating the invisible soul.

Thomas, via Ouija, painted a vivid story full of specific details about his life in the 1800s. This included hard work and dedication to his parish, whom he had loved. Ultimately, however, he revealed that the hands of a jealous young man had taken his life.

At the climax of the story, just as Thomas shared the gruesome details about being murdered brutally with an ax by his assailant, the burning candle suddenly blew out. All by itself. All four of us were startled. We gasped in unison at the timing of the mysterious, creepy incident. Goosebumps covered my body. I felt like someone, or something, was actually in the room hovering over me. Oppressing me. The oxygen was being sucked out of the air. I was completely freaked out and accused my roommates again of pranking me. However, I secretly feared we were messing around with something or someone we shouldn't be.

My roommates also enjoyed playing with tarot cards.

They didn't regard them as a game either. In fact, they made most of their big life decisions with the assistance of the illustrated pictures. Despite my anxious feelings, I allowed the Wiccan to perform a reading on me one day. I figured some insights about my future might prove to be helpful.

After flipping through the cards for a moment, she announced I was going to meet a man soon who would immediately fall in love with me. She described him with many specific details including; long blond hair, a tall slender body, and musical talent. After having first-hand experience with her witchcraft, I didn't scoff at her prediction. In fact, I was hopeful she was right! I was desperate for someone to love me, even if it meant trusting in some hocus pocus.

A few days later, I went to a club in Murfreesboro where we frequently went to watch local bands perform. In between sets the lead singer, who also played guitar, sat next to me at the bar. He introduced himself as Jerry. He was tall, thin, and had long blond hair. He perfectly resembled every detail of the man my roommate recently described. I had never seen him before, and he didn't know my roommates either. In fact, he lived in Nashville, and this gig was his first visit to Murfreesboro. As we talked, I tried to convince myself that our chance meeting wasn't anything special. Besides, he had only introduced himself to me; it didn't mean anything. I chastised myself for being so gullible and chalked it up as coincidence.

Once Jerry finished entertaining the crowd that night, he crossed the crowded room to speak with me again. This time he asked for my phone number and said he wanted to take me out sometime. I almost choked on my beer! I was more than a little freaked out. However, I agreed to his invitation, assuming it was destiny.

Jerry and I hit it off well. He took me to watch his band perform in different clubs around Nashville. We started spending all our time together. However, it was a challenge for us to see each other since I lived in Murfreesboro and he lived on the west side of Nashville over an hour away. Not to mention, I no longer had a car. I was struggling to take care of myself since my parents had quit helping me. My portion of rent and utilities took almost all of small paychecks. I was only left with a humble amount of pocket change to eat with each week. When Jerry offered to let me borrow his car for school and work if I moved in with him, I agreed.

His rusty old car had over 200,000 miles on it. In fact, he said it had even been submerged in the swamps of Florida at one point. It wasn't very reliable to say the least. I drove back and forth across town for a few weeks but the car just couldn't handle the brutal daily commute. I ended up broken-down and stranded on the side of the road many times, usually in the middle of the night. When I got stranded, I was really stranded. If I couldn't wave down a good samaritan for help, I either had to hitchhike or walk several miles to find a pay phone.

Being paranoid didn't mix well with constantly being stuck somewhere alone in the middle of the night. Anger, rage, and paranoia continued to brew inside. I hated myself, and the world, for the terrifying predicaments I kept finding myself in. I was ready to do almost anything to change my circumstances.

Seeing no other reasonable options, I gave up on my aspirations of graduating with a commercial art degree and dropped out of college. I also quit my job bagging groceries in

Murfreesboro and found a new job cleaning hotel rooms in Nashville instead. I still didn't make much money, but I unloaded the stress of having to meet tuition payments and a long, lonely commute.

I wasn't happy with my decision to leave school with only a year left until graduation. I didn't want to be a quitter, but I felt defeated. My parent's option to move back home still stood, but it felt completely unreasonable to me. I just couldn't entertain the idea because I knew I couldn't change my lifestyle to appease them. Moving back home wouldn't solve any problems. I figured it would only create more stress and drama. I took a gamble and banked everything on Jerry instead.

Soon after moving in with Jerry I experienced some real bizarre activity in our house. Random loud noises often came from inside a closet that sounded like something had fallen off a shelf. However, whenever I inspected it nothing was out of order. Friends who spent time in our house also complained about suspicious activity and suggested we had a ghost.

One night, loud repetitive banging suddenly awakened me from sleep. It sounded like someone pounding violently on our front door. The knocking was so strong and persistent it really scared me. Whoever it was seemed desperate for us to answer.

Just as I sat up and tried to discern what was going on, Jerry ran past the front of the bed to go investigate. Motionless, I waited in the dark as my heart pounded inside my chest. I was grateful for his bravery but desperately longed to hear him say everything was okay.

It got quiet. Eerily quiet. Fear swallowed me whole as I

waited and wondered what happened. Finally, I called out, "Jerry? Who is it? What happened?"

At that moment, Jerry sat straight up in the bed beside me where he had been sleeping the whole time. I totally freaked out! I just knew I had seen him walk right in front of me to check on the disturbance.

I became frantic. I whispered, "Somebody is in our house!" I pushed him to get up and search around. I was certain a man had been watching me from the foot of our bed. Jerry turned on all the lights and looked around the house, inside and out. Nobody was there.

I found no good explanation, other than I had seen a ghost, or perhaps, a demon. A horrible feeling came over me. The disembodied apparition was probably not the famously friendly Casper the cartoon ghost. At that moment, I recalled all the strange experiences with the Ouija board and tarot cards and became even more terrified. Not only did crazy people and an angry God want to hurt me; I had demons in hot pursuit too!

While searching through my closet the next day, I found a Bible my mother had given me years before. It had been packed away in a cardboard box and never even looked at. I opened it and decided to read a few Scriptures out loud just like I'd seen Catholic priests do in scary movies. I warned the unseen demons that they weren't allowed to bother me anymore. I felt as if I were in the midst of a hellacious battle and wanted the demons to know I was aligned with the good side, even if it weren't quite true.

The bizarre incidents stopped briefly after openly declaring that my home belonged to Christ. This struck me as an odd coincidence. For me, it further validated the existence of angels and demons and an invisible God. I kept the Bible open in my house for a long time and often read a verse out loud whenever I walked by, you know, just in case.

Being haunted by demons and angry spirits, whether real or just a result of my drug-induced dysfunctional paranoia, I decided to steer clear of anything that might invite evil into my life. Thorny weeds of fear were choking out all hope I had left for a better life.

Desperately longing for safety and security, I convinced myself to try a lot harder to do good things with my life. I thought, *Maybe, just maybe, God might forgive me one day if I shape up.* I bit my lip, pulled up my boot straps again, and set out with renewed vigor and relentless determination to get my life together. Before it was too late.

CHAPTER FOURTEEN

Battling the Grim Reaper

—————◆—————

INDEPENDENCE TURNED OUT to be a lot harder than I expected. The personal freedom I fought so hard for left me with more responsibility and stress than I knew how to manage! I struggled to care for myself. It was a battle to stay healthy—much less thrive, grow, or become all I was meant to be. The world demanded more than I was able to give. Without the college degree I wanted, I barely made a living—not to mention being a cleaning lady wasn't even close to what I wanted to do for the rest of my life. Believe me, I'm grateful for the ones who enjoy the job and do it well. However, my stomach just couldn't handle it.

Cleaning rooms at a skanky hotel on the poor side of town was physically demanding and oftentimes downright disgusting. The overnight visitors weren't the typical out-of-state tourists visiting Music City in hopes of seeing their favorite country star. Instead, the most frequent customers at our hotel were usually local druggies, prostitutes, and wandering hobos.

It's unfathomable that some human beings can live as ghastly as they do. I mean, why would anyone in their right mind smear feces on a wall? It's true! I cleaned other rooms that were beyond all rational explanation as well.

Upon entering one room after checkout one morning, my stomach immediately revolted at the horrendous scene in front of me. The bed linens, towels, and tabletops were splattered with blood. Several used hypodermic needles were haphazardly tossed all over the floor. It was despicable. My instincts told me to run, but I needed the cash so I pressed forward to complete my chore in spite of my repulsion.

I was too desperate and hungry to be picky about my job. Besides, drugs were often left behind by visitors. Many times I pocketed things like morphine and Valium pills, which I considered a nice bonus for all my hard work. Even so, I was growing sick of the twisted, shameful world that I was exposed to every day. I desperately wanted to make something better of myself.

I shared my lofty dreams with coworkers about escaping the daily hell we lived inside the hotel. They all seemed satisfied with their lot though, so I didn't find much encouragement. In fact, my supervisor thought I should be more grateful for the job because it was by far the best she had ever had. I imagine that was true because she also made pornographic films with a group of college boys for extra money. She hated her vulgar side job, but it was quick, easy money. Money that was necessary to maintain her heroin addiction and raise her son.

Another coworker was missing half her teeth and the few remaining ones were rotten black stumps. Her paychecks supported what I assumed to be a crack or meth addiction. Toking on glass pipes full of amphetamines usually left a user's mouth in that kind of deplorable condition. She was kind though and often shared whatever left-behind stash she found from hotel visitors with me.

My best friend at the hotel was a girl my age who was always scheduled for the same shift. We took all our smoke breaks together. On top of drinking and drugging, I had a pretty nasty cigarette habit at the time too. I could easily finish a pack or more a day. So we took frequent breaks by the dumpster in the back parking lot.

During one of our breaks, she said she wanted to divulge a personal secret to me. I was intrigued. I never would have predicted what followed though. She proudly proclaimed that she was Wiccan and asked if I knew what that was. Unfortunately, I knew exactly what she meant since I had recently experienced some pretty creepy things while living with my Murfreesboro roomies.

Then, in a matter-of-fact, nonchalant way, my coworker informed me she had recently cast a voodoo spell on a guy which actually killed him, just as she had intended. She didn't have to say much to convince me that evil spirits and black magic were real. I believed her. However, the thought of someone casting spells to murder people intensified my paranoia about what demons wanted to do to me.

I didn't let on that I was afraid. I wanted her to see me as an ally. But I secretly feared that Satan was pursuing me. Relentlessly. Even mocking me by using her to inform me that he had every intention of destroying me.

I assumed if I had more money, then I could live in a better area and escape the addiction and depravity that I was immersed in. Therefore, I took on a second job as a maid for several wealthy families on the nice side town near my childhood stomping grounds. Their homes were luxurious compared to the horrifying filth of the hotel. However, the job was still backbreaking toil. The well-to-do homeowners expected their toilets and tubs to literally sparkle and shine; every surface left perfectly spotless. That could only be accomplished by using an old toothbrush to reach every crevice and crease and required a lot of elbow grease. By the time I got home each day I was flat-out exhausted.

Much to my surprise and disappointment, Jerry didn't hold a regular job. He never provided much, if any, financial support towards our expenses. He put his whole life into music and felt entitled to spend his days writing and nights performing. Gigs in Music City typically didn't pay unless you were able to collect tips or a cover charge from the handful of people that actually showed up. I wasn't fond of the arrangement, but his daily profession of love was priceless to me so I provided for the two of us the best I could. I even wanted to see his dreams come true as much as he did.

I can honestly say I ate more ramen noodles and canned tuna than the average of all college students and low-income families combined. I was so poor that getting a free cup of ice from the gas station was a real treat because I didn't even own a refrigerator. I eventually bought a small, used toaster oven to heat up food, but that was it as far as appliances. I certainly didn't have cable TV or any other luxuries like air conditioning. Our run-down shack didn't have much furniture either. I hung old, dirty blankets over the windows for curtains. The house simply provided shelter, and that was fine by me. It was mine; I worked really hard for it.

A couple of years later, I added a third job to my routine. I was tired of pinching pennies and still being hungry. Life was too uncomfortable. Barely scraping by didn't allow me any simple pleasures in life like a new pair of shoes, an occasional hamburger, or even a haircut. So I had to work more. The sad truth about addiction is it becomes your priority over food, water, and other necessities.

Eventually I found a print company that was looking for a contractor to do some grunt work. They loaned me a machine to laminate hotel service directories for five cents apiece. Basically my job was to take their printed materials and feed them through the machine, then trim off any excess plastic around the edges. Once laminated, the covers could be bound with their interior contents and shipped to hotels. It was quite boring and time consuming but it did allow me to work at home whenever I had free time. It was a perfect third job since I could squeeze it in between my other two work schedules.

I made a whopping $12,000 a year while I worked three strenuous jobs. I felt rich too. I finally had enough money to cover rent and groceries. I even bought an occasional Cornish hen and cooked it in my tiny toaster oven for a real treat. This made me feel like a wealthy queen at a royal feast. Compared to the canned meat products and soup that had been my primary menu items for several years, it really was.

Jerry took me to every performance his band played around Nashville. I made friends with a lot of other musicians and club owners around town. I wasn't old enough to be inside the bars drinking, but nobody ever complained since I was with the band. I refused to be seen as a groupie though, so I volunteered to help the band any way I could.

I became the band's graphic designer and photographer. I created art for demo tapes, made posters to advertise upcoming shows, and took photos for write-ups in the local newspaper. I also learned how to run the light board during gigs. Knowing their songs made it easy to punch color changes to go along with the music or to give someone a spotlight for their solo. Changing broken guitar strings and packing gear before and after each show also became part of my regular duties. I actually felt like another member of the band.

While my days were long and grueling with physical labor, my nights were full of excitement and creativity. I seized every opportunity to learn a new skill, hoping to get my life into better shape. Things seemed to be going well.

One of the perks, or so I thought at the time, of being with a talented musician in Nashville was the abundance of free alcohol and drugs. During every show the club managers and fans would buy us drinks and various other substances. We never declined an offer to party. During that time my daily bad habits escalated to a whole new level. I felt entitled to a good time after working so hard so I indulged more than ever.

Eventually word got around about my artistic skill set and I earned the opportunity to photograph several other bands around town. Because everyone in the music business seemed to be low on cash, but high on drugs, I usually bartered my creative services in exchange for getting wasted. It's crazy that I could barely afford beans and rice, yet I had more marijuana, cocaine, and alcohol than I could handle.

I got so much work freelancing and taking photos that I eventually set up a dark room in my bathroom; thanks to a friend who loaned me the needed equipment in exchange for work. I began developing film and prints myself. I finally felt like my life was on the right track and headed somewhere good. Despite the fact I dropped out of college, I had stumbled onto a way to pursue my creative dreams, and I was proud of myself.

The long strenuous days and nights of work, coupled with constant alcohol and drug use, led my young body to become completely worn down in short time. I wasn't eating well. I wasn't sleeping. There was never time to relax. My life was in overdrive all the time. I lost so much weight I was rail thin with yellow eyes. My long, brittle hair hadn't been cut in years. My skin was so sickly pale that I made vampires look tan. I was undernourished from lack of vitamins and minerals and overindulged in everything toxic.

I decided to quit one of my three jobs so I could enjoy a more relaxed tempo with some occasional down time. Even so, the change required my income to be supplemented somehow. That's when Jerry and I started selling marijuana to fill the financial gap.

Selling pot was great at first. Once we purchased our initial investment the business was up and running. We made our money back in just a couple of days. It was easy money because all the business came to us. Plus, we always had return customers! In just a few transactions we earned the same amount of money that a week of cleaning toilets and scrubbing bathtubs would make. Most of our buyers were other local musicians, but over time our clientele grew to include their friends and acquaintances. Business was booming!

In fact, business was booming so much that people were

constantly over at our house. I began to fear the traffic would make neighbors suspicious and someone would alert the cops. It was quite annoying too because every time I laid down to rest someone else would knock on the door—at all hours of the day and night. Our exchanges were never quick either. Most buyers insisted on sampling the product by taking hits from our two-foot tall glass bong before investing. It created a persistent haze of thick smoke that lingered in the air all the time. I never found the peace I longed for after quitting one of my jobs, but the money coming in was a lot better.

In order to stay awake when overly exhausted, I became even more dependent on cocaine and caffeine pills. Coke was also the drug of choice by most club owners took so it was shared with us more frequently than anything else. Whenever we had extra cash flow from selling quarter bags of weed, we usually pitched in with friends and bought eight balls of the energizing white powder. Mixing cocaine with alcohol and marijuana felt great too. I was more stable and less frenzied while using them together which allowed me to party for longer periods of time.

On my twenty-third birthday we had one of our typical all-night parties. It started around midnight at our house after a gig. We had already been drinking for several hours at the club before the party even started. As we sat on the floor around our small coffee table, my friends and I sang songs together while cutting up lines of cocaine and taking turns smoking the bong in between snorts.

That night one of my friends showed me how to cook cocaine in a spoon with water and baking soda to separate the freebase into a rock that could be smoked. Within seconds of taking my first toke off a pipe of homemade crack, I felt a powerful rush. It felt like I had the ability to run through brick walls without being hurt. I envisioned myself fighting an army of ninjas all by myself and coming out victorious! In my imagination, I reigned supreme over the piles of masked enemies that were lying in heaps around me. The rush of courage empowered me with an amazing amount of confidence. It felt great compared to my typical paranoid state.

By the next morning, I had consumed more alcohol, marijuana, and cocaine than I had ever done before. I knew my body couldn't take any more. I walked outside to enjoy some fresh air as the sun began to rise. Instead of taking in a breath of rejuvenating oxygen, I was suddenly overcome by an odd, incredibly disturbing, sensation.

After a moment of extreme vertigo, it suddenly felt like my soul was outside of my body. I was actually looking back at my disheveled body which wavered back and forth like it was about to fall. The out-of-body delusion lasted for several seconds. But just as quickly as the experience started, I was zapped back inside myself. The sudden pain and discomfort of being inside my body again was creepy and disorienting. Frantically, my eyes searched back and forth for evidence to explain what was going on. I felt sick. Violently sick. It wasn't the same kind of nausea that typically accompanied drinking too much liquor. Rather, it felt like I was dying.

My heart was beating too fast. My body was caving in on itself. I tried everything I could to calm down. I took slow deep breaths in and out. It brought no relief. I went back inside the house, fell on my bed, and tried to rest. Lying still only made me feel worse. I got up and tried pacing around in circles to match the frantic rhythm of my heart. I tried jumping up and down. I tried eating. Nothing helped. I only felt worse with each second that went by.

Dying was not a pleasant experience! I writhed in agony for several torturous hours while the Grim Reaper reached his long deadly fingers inside my body, grabbed onto my soul, and tried to snatch it from me. My ears rang with echoes of demonic growling voices that mocked me with laughter throughout the whole experience. I knew I was being dragged straight into hell.

I should have had someone rush me to the emergency room, but it never even occurred to me as an option in my delirious state. Not to mention, I couldn't afford emergency services and didn't have medical insurance. I certainly didn't want to end up getting arrested. All I could think of was finding a place to be alone, where I could emphatically plead with God for my life. For the first time, I got on my knees and prayed with earnest, sincere desperation.

God, I know I have been making bad decisions. I know I have disobeyed you and my parents. I know I'm about to die. I don't want to go like this. Please. Please don't let me die. My parents will be crushed. I can't let my brother and sister see me like this. Lord! Please! Help me! I promise to stop living like this if you keep me alive. Please! Don't let it end like this.

I didn't want to be buried at the age of twenty-three. I knew God held the keys to life and death, so I begged him to spare me from the demons that joyfully taunted my demise. I agonized through prayer for several long hours that night. I prayed and prayed and prayed until my heart finally slowed down and I was able to breathe normally again.

Being so intimately confronted by death was the most unsettling and difficult experience of my life. I knew God had spared me because He was good and certainly not because I deserved it. I wasn't sure why He answered my prayers for safety and survival since I was so rebellious towards Him. Yet, because He had rescued me from the clutches of an eternity in hell, I wanted to keep my end of the bargain.

I was worried that God wouldn't believe me though. Many promises to do better had been broken before. Crossing my fingers, I vowed to give sobriety and obedience my best shot because I knew I had been given my very last chance.

I don't know how I'm going do it God, so I need you to help me get off drugs. Somehow. Anyhow. Do whatever it takes!

CHAPTER FIFTEEN

The Power of Provision

———————◆———————

I HAVE LEARNED over the years never to underestimate a mother's intuition. While my mom had no knowledge of the numerous horrifying details of my life, she always knew something was wrong. Even when I wasn't honest with her, she knew better. I believe a large part of her intuition is due to her constant communication with God. She endlessly prayed on my behalf. My downward trajectory profoundly grieved her as she watched me abandon every principle she and my father had taught me as a child. I was more than a disappointment. I was a source of dissension and drama for my whole family.

I avoided seeing my family as much as possible while I spiraled into the hellacious abyss and squandered my life away. I couldn't face the pain I saw in their eyes whenever we met. On major holidays like Christmas, guilt compelled me to call or at least stop by for a brief visit but that was it.

My diminishing health always alarmed my mother, and

she constantly pleaded with me to come home. My dysfunctional perceptions never allowed me to see her desire to keep me safe as love. Rather, I perceived it as a threat to what little control I had in my life. I was just too stubborn and prideful to admit defeat.

I never accepted any invitations to church either. I thought for sure the shiny, happy people club (which I believed Christians belonged to) would reject me. There were far too many filthy things I had seen and done. Despite thousands of rejected invitations, my parents never stopped asking.

Eventually my parent's prayers became seriously desperate. They begged God to intervene in my life however He could—good *or bad*. They were even willing to sacrifice their own life; if it meant mine would turn around.

Soon after their "do whatever it takes" appeal to God my dad was diagnosed with colon cancer. Mom was torn with emotions the day she found out. On one hand, Dad was sick and needed radical surgery to prolong his jeopardized life. The future was full of uncertainty. On the other hand, she assumed it was the big life event that would finally bring me home.

My father spent three long months at Baptist Hospital in Nashville while he fought for his life. I only went to visit him once. It was too hard to see the strong man I knew lying helpless in bed. He had lost eighty pounds and was no more than a frail bag of bones wrapped in loose, sunken skin; literally a shell of the man that used to be the invincible disciplinarian I grew up with. I barely even recognized him.

The doctors performed three surgeries to remove a grapefruit-sized tumor in Dad's abdomen. They also removed two feet of intestines, his spleen, gall bladder, and half of his pancreas. As a way to manage pain, he was attached to a morphine drip that he could self-administer. During my visit his pain was so intense, he took too much of the body numbing painkiller and his heart stopped beating. Code Blue alerts rang throughout the hospital halls while doctors scurried to revive him.

As I stood there watching my father die, I knew what a disappointment I had been to him. It was unbearably painful. It grieved me that our relationship was ending the way it was —broken.

Despite his deteriorating condition, Mom turned her focus to me. She began to read Bible verses out loud and plead for me to give my life to Christ. I guess she thought there was no better time to discuss death and the afterlife than during Dad's Code Blue. She seemed to be more distraught over my life than his, as if I were the one dying. Or maybe I was a just a good distraction from the stress of watching him suffer. Or perhaps it's because she had peace with him knowing his eternal life was secure. She knew he would be in heaven after his last breath. As for me, I was destined straight for hell which grieved her far more than anything else.

I was offended that her focus was on me while a team of doctors and nurses scurried to work on my dad. The frenzy of activity to keep him breathing was all I could focus on. There was no need for her to remind me how bad things were. I already knew. In fact, my life was a thousand times worse than she could even imagine! Besides, I had promised God I was going to change, and I was determined to do it. Without her help.

After several frantic moments, the doctors managed to

revive my father and get him stabilized again. I was so relieved. He was still alive.

As a part of Dad's recovery plan, the doctors said he needed to undergo chemotherapy for a year. Even so, they believed he only had a small chance to live another five years. Somehow he miraculously survived the life threatening ordeal and brutal chemical routines like child's play. His determination won the battle over death which astonished everyone on his medical team. It's been over twenty years now, and he's still going strong! I guess I got my stubborn tenacity from him.

At the same time my father was struggling in the hospital, my brother's wedding day was coming. Rodney had proposed to his college girlfriend, Tammy, several months prior to my dad's cancer diagnosis, so the timing of their big day was unfortunate.

Against the doctor's wishes, my father insisted on traveling to the ceremony. He was too frail to walk or stand. Plus, his wounds needed to be cleaned and dressed several times a day. The doctor agreed to release him for the wedding *only* if we found a wheelchair accessible van to travel in, and if we had someone trained to care for him on the journey.

My mother searched for ways to make his attendance possible while my sister and I got fitted for our bridesmaid's dresses. I wasn't looking forward to the family reunion. I was afraid all my relatives would cast judgmental glances towards me for my deplorable lifestyle. Regardless, I swallowed my pride by convincing myself I didn't really care what they thought anyway.

A few days before the wedding, I suddenly began to feel nauseated and sick. I assumed it was a result of the stress over my father's health mixed with dread over the certain interrogation I would be under once my family was together. Then I realized another unusual and alarming symptom; I missed my period.

Uh oh! I hope that doesn't mean what I think it means!

The curiosity to know if I was pregnant was killing me. I couldn't wait to find out for sure, so I gathered as much loose change as I could find and headed to the nearest pharmacy. Coins jangled in my pocket because I nervously played with them while I stood in the aisle and picked out a pregnancy test kit.

What if I am pregnant? What will I do? I haven't even been able to take care of myself very well. How in the world am I going to take care of a baby?

Somehow I knew what the test results were going to be. I was right; it was positive.

Really? Me? Right now? On top of everything else? Really God?

My mind filled with hundreds of questions, none of which I knew the answers to.

How can I afford to have a baby? Am I even healthy enough to have a normal baby? Oh crap! My plan to wean off drugs is never going to work now. God, I thought you were going to help me! What am I going to do?

My feelings of desperation sank to a whole new level.

I was nervous to share my news with Jerry. I wasn't sure what his response would be. Having a baby would require major lifestyle changes for both of us and it wasn't going to be easy. When I finally mustered up the nerve to inform him about his new role as a father, he seemed supportive but nervous. He even suggested we get married.

I was happily surprised. I knew everything would be okay as long as Jerry was there to help. A few days later he gave me an engagement ring that had been worn by his dear grandmother once upon a time. His sentimental gift was a comfort and raised my level of confidence that all would be fine. We even made plans for a simple wedding. My nervousness was replaced with excitement about becoming a family.

This is going to be great! This is exactly what we needed to get our lives in order. I'm ready!

Over the next several days, I questioned Jerry with every concern I had. There was so much to do to prepare for the baby's arrival. I didn't want to sell drugs or stay out all night partying anymore. I also didn't want shady people visiting our house at all hours of the night. It just didn't seem right to bring a helpless infant into the environment we currently lived in. I asked him to get a job and help with the bills since we needed diapers and other baby related necessities. There was no way I could afford everything by myself.

Rather than share my concerns, or even help develop a plan of action, Jerry became quiet. He seemed to grow more and more agitated with each question as if they were impositions. He eventually snapped by responding with one quick question back to me, "Have you considered an abortion?"

"An abortion? Seriously? You want me to kill our baby?" I was hysterical.

I cried, "Of course I haven't considered an abortion. Just because I wasn't ready to have a kid, doesn't mean I should get rid of it! How could you even suggest something like that?"

My heart shattered into a million pieces. He continued to mumble quietly under his breath but I heard him say, "Why is it that only the woman has a choice?"

In that moment I realized Jerry didn't have our baby's best interest at heart. I was scared, confused, and totally heartbroken. All my hopes for turning our lives around and becoming a happy little family came to a screeching halt.

Meanwhile, it was time to travel to Alabama for Rodney's wedding. I was only six weeks pregnant so I was relieved to fit into my bridesmaid dress. Nobody would be able to tell. My father was still gravely ill but had fortunately found someone who loaned him the kind of van he needed to travel safely. My father's best friend even volunteered to clean and dress his wounds and be of assistance to my mother during the event. I was amazed at how people willingly jumped in to care for him during the unusual challenge. I desperately longed for the same kind of people in my life— people who loved me so much they would do whatever they could to help.

I was on the verge of tears throughout the whole wedding. I was happy for my brother, but also very jealous. I wanted my parents to rejoice and celebrate my big life event too, but I feared it would severely disappoint them once they found out. I decided to wait until we got home and take one more pregnancy test, just to be sure, before I told them they were going to be grandparents.

The wedding was beautiful. Dad was too weak to stand and perform his role in the ceremony, so Papa stood in as best man. As he sat slouched in his wheelchair at the base of the stage, he appeared to be suffering greatly. Nonetheless, he forced a smile under sunken eyes to show support for my brother. There wasn't a dry eye in the whole church for those who witnessed the remarkable display of affection my father made for his only son. I realized that day that he would literally give his life for us, and I wanted to make him proud of me too.

When I got back home, a second test confirmed that I was indeed pregnant. I couldn't avoid the inevitable forever and needed to tell my parents. On Easter morning 1992, I called them. I'm not sure why I picked the religious holiday to deliver my news other than I hoped their hearts would be softened towards me on the special day. Much to my surprise, my mother didn't go on a tirade like I expected. She didn't even act surprised. Rather, she seemed almost relieved and eager to help.

Over the next several months my mother ensured I ate well by providing me with healthy food and vitamins. She also took me to every doctor appointment I needed. Her ongoing support helped me realize how much she really did care about me. I knew she had my best interest at heart, unlike anybody else I knew.

During the pregnancy, something truly miraculous began to happen within my body. It was nothing short of divine intervention. Apart from the miracle of a growing child inside, I was able to quit smoking and drinking with ease. The stronghold of addiction, which had enslaved me for so many years, simply dissipated. In fact, my body was repulsed at the smell, or thought, of those toxic substances. Having a growing baby inside my body, who was dependent on me for life, physically changed the insidious cravings. The only things I ached for were proper nutrition and clean air. I was sober for the first time in a decade. God was answering my prayers to overcome addiction in a truly remarkable way.

During the fifth month of pregnancy my mother took me for an ultrasound. I was eager to learn the baby's gender so I could settle on a name and buy clothes. The nurse pointed to a turtle-shaped shadow on the fuzzy black and white photos and confirmed I was having a son. I had been hoping for a son. The fear of having a girl, who might go through some of the same challenges I had, rattled me to the core. I earnestly begged God for a strong boy, and He came through. Again!

After the brief celebration from the doctor's announcement, he said he had additional news for me. The doctor said the placenta was positioned below the baby near the birth canal and not above him like it was supposed to be. He explained that the condition, known as placenta previa, posed a serious threat to both of our lives. As the baby grew and moved around, the weight on the placenta could cause me to hemorrhage. If that were to happen I could bleed to death rather quickly as well as endanger the baby. The doctor ordered me to stop working immediately and demanded 24/7 bed rest for the remainder of my term with no exceptions.

I have to quit working? How in the world am I going to have a baby without a job? God, why would you do this to me? I thought things were getting better. This is going to be impossible now!

When I got home that afternoon I shared the doctor's diagnosis with Jerry. While describing the risks, I desperately appealed for him to take over providing for our financial needs. His response shocked me. I knew he would be stressed, but I didn't expect what happened. He was furious. He refused to be forced into that position. He showed no concern for my health. I don't even think he believed me about the diagnosis. I felt completely deserted and distraught. Alone. Hopeless.

Is this some sort of cruel joke, God? How could things possibly get any worse?

I decided that day to apply for welfare and food stamps. It was the only reasonable option that came to mind. I went to the government office downtown and filled out the required paperwork to receive assistance. It wasn't enough money to clothe or care for my son when he arrived, or even enough to pay rent, but it was enough to cover the critical essentials at that time—food and water.

A few weeks later, on my twenty-fourth birthday, there was an unexpected knock on my front door. When I opened the door an angry man stood on my porch. He informed me that all of our neighbors were complaining about the knee-high jungle of weeds growing in front of my house. In a firm and condescending tone he demanded I mow my yard immediately. If I didn't comply, I would be fined, my landlord would be notified, and I would be asked to move out. Things did get worse.

I was six months pregnant and under strict orders to stay in bed. I had no lawnmower and no money to hire anyone to help. It was also a blistering hot summer day. The sauna like heat alone made me feel sick. Jerry wasn't home either. The closer it got to our son's expected birth date the more he stayed out partying with friends. I stood there inside my rundown shack of a house, all by myself, and cried out loud.

Lord, if you really care about me then I need your help! Please! What am I supposed to do? Things keep getting worse. I can't do this by myself anymore. I need you!

No joke, just a few minutes later a friend drove up my driveway and said, "I happened to see this cheap lawnmower at a garage sale I drove by and thought you could use it. Happy Birthday." I'm sure they were too embarrassed to hang out in my forest of weeds, so they left the lawnmower and went on their way. I literally lost my breath at the incredible timing of their gift. I was completely shocked. In awe.

That was an incredible coincidence!

Just as I had that thought, guilt convicted me to change my response.

Okay, maybe it wasn't a coincidence; it had to be a miracle. God, you answered my prayer. Thank you for the lawnmower. But how am I supposed to take care of this thick overgrown brush by myself? I can't risk losing my child or my home. Nice trick, but I am still in a hopeless situation here. I can't do this by myself.

As amazed as I was by God's divine provision, I still felt confused and afraid. I wasn't sure what to do next; as if God hadn't thought His plan out completely. I decided to start mowing anyways. I convinced myself to take it real slow and stop for a break between each pass across the yard. With little effort, the lawnmower started right up, and I set out to accomplish the daunting task.

I immediately realized the job would have been more effectively tackled with a machete. It was far more difficult than I could handle in my condition. I was completely overwhelmed and humiliated. Defeated. I began to break down standing right there in my front yard. I had no idea how I was going to build a future for my son living the way I was. There was nobody to depend on for help. I was desperate.

Okay, okay, okay God. I get it. I can't do this. I GIVE UP!

As I cried out towards the sky a young boy about twelve years old appeared out of nowhere and said, "Ma'am, I'd like to finish mowing your lawn for you if that's okay." I was completely awestruck. My knees buckled. I was in shock.

As I watched him complete the arduous yard work through my window, tears poured like a waterfall from my eyes. For the first time in my life, I was fully aware that God had His giant, loving arms around me. Despite my constant running away and broken promises, He continued to pursue me and care for me. I was embarrassed at my arrogance for believing I was the one in control of all things. I acknowledged His great provision by saying, "I don't know why you want to take care of me the way you do, but you have my full attention."

God wasn't done showing off for me either. A few weeks later my mother called and said some ladies at her church wanted to throw a baby shower for me. I was reluctant to go at first. I couldn't understand why a group of strangers wanted to have a party for me. But, I needed all the help I could get. At that point, I would have done almost anything for free diapers so I agreed to go.

My grandmother made a nice maternity dress for me to wear at the party, but I was still embarrassed to show up as the center of attention. I was dirt poor, young, pregnant, and unmarried. I was insecure and afraid of their judgment. When I got there, I was flabbergasted by the number of women and the huge pile of presents waiting for me.

Why would they do this for me? I don't even know them. God, why do you continue to bless me when I've been so rebellious?

Everyone at the party was friendly and didn't snub their

noses like I had predicted. Instead, they were eager to celebrate the arrival of my son with me. They gave me a lot more than free diapers too. They blessed me with dozens of outfits, toys, a bathtub, a stroller, a car seat, and even a baby bed! It was everything I would ever need to take care of my son.

I was in awe at the kindness of strangers. They even served me fresh fruit and sandwiches. I felt like a real queen as I relaxed in a fancy, cushioned armchair with my feet propped up. Their generosity humbled me so much that I longed to become a different person. It made me want to be kind and generous to others one day too.

God had my attention. I knew He was up to something, but I wasn't sure what it was. He had performed miracles and lavished me gifts, all while I gave nothing in return. I spent the next several months pondering why.

God, why would you want to give me what I don't deserve? If you're so great, why do you pursue ME of all people? I am nothing, nobody. I have squandered my life and lived in completed defiance. I have broken every promise I made to you. I disobeyed you and my parents over and over and over again. I'm broken, worthless, used, abused, filthy, and impure. Don't you know what's happened to me? Don't you know what I've done? What would the God of the universe want from little ole messed up me?

Then, like a soft, warm blanket taken right out of the laundry room dryer, I felt God's incredible love come over me. He said, "I have plans for you."

CHAPTER SIXTEEN

The Dissolution of Self

I WAS SCHEDULED to have a C-section at the end of November 1992. As much as I tried to follow the doctor's orders and stay in bed, there were too many things to do in preparation for my son's arrival. Most importantly, the thick perma-fog and smoke residue that lingered in the sheets, clothes, and curtains needed cleaning. I was determined to have a safe environment for my son when he came home for the first time.

One evening, just as I began doing some laundry, I started to feel nauseated. A swirling dizziness forced me to stop what I was doing. We were three weeks away from my scheduled procedure, so I decided to heed the doctor's advice and take it easy. Disappointed that my home wasn't as ready I felt it should be, I decided to relax by going out for pizza. There I could listen to a friend play the piano while enjoying dinner. Besides, a date night out with Jerry might help me feel better.

Soon after we started eating I began to have cramps and felt sick again. Assuming I just needed to relieve some pressure from my bladder, I went to the restroom. That's when I unexpectedly discovered blood.

Oh no! This is what the doctor warned me about. This isn't good! I'm going to hemorrhage!

I immediately ran to Jerry and said, "We have to go to the hospital, right now! I'm bleeding. It's an emergency! Let's go, let's go, let's go!" Thankfully he complied. We immediately got in the car and sped down the highway. Jerry's rusty old car barreled down the road towards Baptist Hospital as fast it could go.

Please, Lord, help us get there in time. Please, Lord!

When we arrived at the emergency room, I hobbled inside and told the lady at the front desk I was bleeding. When she noticed how pregnant I was she immediately swept into action. Instantaneously, a whole slew of frenzied nurses surrounded me before I even had time to blink. One nurse hooked me to an IV while another frantically shaved my belly while another attached a monitor to listen to the baby's heart. They performed their various tasks with such speed and efficiency that NASCAR pit crews would be impressed.

Thump, thump...pause...thump...pause...thump, thump, thump, thump...pause.

His heartbeat was irregular. The nurses yelled at one another that the baby was distressed. He needed to come out right away. They scrambled around me like an army of ants whose home had been poked with a stick.

I began another desperate plea to God.

Lord, please help me! Please save my baby! Please! I'm sorry I didn't follow all the rules. Please don't punish my son for my disobedience. Please save him!

Within ten minutes of my arrival at the emergency room, I was examined and fully prepped for surgery. I was amazed at how fast they moved to take care of me although the seriousness of my situation was alarming. As I lay on the table in the ER and waited for the doctor, the anesthesiologist hovered over me. With calm, soothing words he described how he was going to administer drugs to knock me out so they could perform an emergency C-section. He said, "By the time you count to three, you will be asleep. The procedure won't take long. I'll wake you up soon, and you can see your child. Are you ready to count?"

One, two…GASP! Choke! I can't breathe. Help. Wait. I can't breathe. Help!!

The anesthesiologist was right. I was knocked out on the count of three, but it wasn't a graceful process. I struggled to breathe, and I was unable to let him know. I tried to grunt or make a sound to indicate I was suffocating to no avail.

I'm choking. Somebody help!

I was terrified with no ability to scream for help.

Don't they know I can't breathe? God help! HELP!

After a terrifying moment of grappling for air, my lungs were finally restored with oxygen, and I began to breathe again.

Ahhh! Thank you. Thank you. Thank you. I'm so glad I can breathe again. That was scary!

Just then I suddenly felt the doctor press down on my uterus.

Ow! I can feel that! Oh no! What's happening? Why can I feel that?

I was fully aware of the activity around me and the

painful surgery my body was undergoing, but I couldn't move.

Hey! I'm here! I'm not unconscious. Please don't start the surgery!

I used all my strength and mental focus to try and move a finger or grunt to let the doctors know I was there. But I couldn't. I was trapped inside my paralyzed body, unable to open my eyes, or make a sound. Without warning, I felt the sharp knife splice its way through my abdomen.

Nooooo! This is horrible! Somebody help!

A few seconds later, I felt the weight of the baby removed from the hole in my gut. The nurses quickly carried him to a nearby table to clean him up. Several voices echoed around the room discussing the bowel movement he had in the womb. They said they needed to clear his airways before major damage was done to his tiny lungs.

What is happening? Why can't I move? I need to see my son!

A moment later, I finally heard the most glorious sound I have ever heard in my life—my son's first cry. The room applauded with joy and praise. He had been rescued just in the nick of time. A single moment longer inside my womb would have seriously compromised his life. They all rejoiced at the miraculous timing of their rescue.

Thank you! Thank you! Thank you!

I celebrated inside my immoveable body with them. I could hardly wait to meet him. My son's time of birth was marked at 11:09 p.m. on November 9, 1992.

Amid the praises for a remarkable delivery, the worse pain of all suddenly flushed over me. The doctor pressed on my empty abdomen and placed multiple staples in to hold my flesh back together and my soul writhed in agony inside my immoveable carcass.

Oh God!!!!!!!!!!

At that moment, I finally lost all consciousness.

A couple of hours later I woke up as a doctor pressed on my abdomen again, but this time it was accompanied by a rush of warm liquid from between my legs. Blood was gushing from me in startling amounts. I opened my eyes and tried to make sense of what was happening.

My eyes darted around the room because I expected the nurse to gently place my newborn son into my arms. He wasn't there. A doctor suddenly hovered above me and gently pressed on my shoulders to force me to lie back down. He informed me that my son was safe with relatives in the nursery. Unfortunately I wouldn't be able to see him until I was stable. I was in the intensive care unit while they tried to control the bleeding.

I'm bleeding to death? No! I need to be a mother to my son! God, please don't let me die. Please!

My parents arrived at the hospital soon after the delivery. They made phone calls to friends and other family members requesting prayers on my behalf. They were excited to hold their healthy grandson but were very concerned for my well-being.

As I lay hemorrhaging and fighting for my life, I earnestly prayed for divine intervention, again.

I promise to be the best mother I can be. Please God. Please believe me this time. Please let me take care of my son! I'll do everything you want me to, if you keep me alive for him.

After several long dramatic hours and the persistent care of good doctors, accompanied by prayers from family and friends, I was finally stabilized enough to meet my son for the first time.

It was the happiest moment of my entire life! The love that overcame me when I first saw him was unlike anything I had ever experienced before. Pain completely dissipated in the wake of pure joy and elation that I felt holding his warm little body against my chest.

He was beautiful. I couldn't stop crying. The nurses even commented about how perfect he was without the misshaped cone head like most newborns have. As I kissed his soft round face for the first time I quietly whispered, "I'm so excited to meet you! I promise to take care of you the best I possibly can, no matter what it takes. You are my angel baby, London. I love you!"

I remained in the hospital for several days until I recovered enough to be released. I was so excited to bring baby London home. Every minute was spent staring at his precious face. I was amazed that I had been blessed with such a wonderful gift—an undeserved perfect gift. I was willing to do anything required to ensure he would grow up safe and healthy.

From day one, London was very alert and inquisitive. He was almost always awake, with eyes wide open as he explored the new world around him. Our favorite thing to do for the first few weeks of his life was lie on the floor underneath the Christmas tree. We'd gaze up into thousands of colorful glimmering lights together while we listened to classical music in the background. The lights flickered in time with the music, which had an incredible calming effect on both of us. I constantly reassured baby London how much I loved him while the glow of his angelic face changed colors under the tree.

In the meantime, Jerry continued to spend a lot of time away with his friends. I had assumed the partying would stop for him too once our son was home, but I was wrong. Night after night, whenever London was asleep, I sat by the window and stared outside into the darkness and waited for him to come home. I was hurt. Longing for something better, I wondered how London and I were going to get by without Jerry's support.

I thought he loved us. Why isn't he here? Doesn't he feel compelled to help?

After three long months I couldn't bear the pain of the lonely nightly routine any longer. Financially, I was in the worst shape I had ever been in my life. My bills were overdue. I had no idea how I was going get a job and care for London at the same time. I was more desperate than ever. Broken by grief, I cried out to God again. He had shown up for me many times before, and I needed His help again. However, this time something very different happened.

When I tossed my wishes up into the air this time, I was suddenly overcome by God's presence. There wasn't an audible voice in the room, but I had the impression that He was right there beside me, emanating with divine power and clarity. Then we had a very real conversation.

Why are you afraid?

Because I'm all alone. I'm scared.

You're not alone. I am right here.

Where is Jerry? I don't think he wants us. What am I going to do without his help?

I will provide for you.

Yes, God. I know you can. You have proven that to me already. I'm just scared. I can't work and care for London at the same time. London needs me right now. How am I supposed to do this?

Why do you doubt me?

I don't understand. My life has been so messed up. Why do you want to help when I have broken so many promises to you? I've done so many things wrong.

I love you. I want a relationship with you.

But my life is still a mess. I haven't gotten everything in order yet. Maybe you should come back in a few months. I'll be ready then. Things are getting better.

I didn't ask you to get things in order first. You need me now.

But, you're God! You're holy and righteous and perfect. I can't let you in. I'm too filthy and disgusting. Why would you want to be anywhere near someone like me?

I love you. I have plans for you and London.

God, I believe in you. I know you exist. But come on, let's get real. I don't think I can carry out any plans for you. I'm a mess. I am nothing. I'm a failure.

I will enable you. Just give your life to me.

But, I do believe in you. Isn't that what you want?

Even demons know I exist. I want you to surrender. Follow me.

I thought I needed to be sinless before I could have a relationship with you.

You are not capable of perfection.

I know! That's why I'm so confused about why you're here!

I wanted to give my life to God, but I was stuck on believing I needed to get myself cleaned up first. He reminded me of all the ways He provided for me, but I remained confused. I couldn't understand why He continued to pursue a relationship with me when I was so worthless.

Why would you want a relationship with someone who has lived such a reckless life? What do you think London and I could possibly do for you? Don't you know my son was born out of wedlock? Don't you know how screwed up my life has been? You are God. What could I possibly do for you?

Despite my doubt about everything God said to me, He was patient and persistent. He kept reminding me that He loved me no matter how many questions I asked.

But God, I really don't think I can be good enough.

At that moment, Jerry stumbled into the house. It was four o'clock in the morning. He was obviously intoxicated. I questioned his whereabouts and told him I was disappointed in his lack of support. I asked why he wouldn't get a job. My questions got no response. Nothing was changing for him. In fact, people continued to show up at our house to buy drugs despite my requests for the business to stop. He even insisted on smoking in the house. He argued that closing London's bedroom door was enough to protect his baby lungs from the thick toxic haze, but I disagreed. I resented him deeply in that moment as he defiantly blew smoke in my face.

Jerry's actions threatened the health and future of our son which made me absolutely livid. That's when mama bear showed up.

Our conversation quickly escalated to a horrible argument. Screams of disappointment filled the air for over an hour while we blamed each other for our sorry lives. I made it very clear I was ready to do whatever I had to do to protect London, even if that meant leaving him.

At that moment Jerry shoved me across the room. I stumbled backwards into a table, which made a large crashing sound against the wall. My disappointment and anger turned to fear. I was shocked. The man I loved, who I thought loved me, would rather hurt me than help.

After getting back to my feet, I threatened to smash his guitar into tiny pieces for loving music more than his own child. Jerry looked at me with angry red eyes and snarled with a vicious murderous voice that actually threatened to kill me if I touched any of his instruments.

This is way out of control. This is bad. This is worse than bad!

I wasn't sure what to do next. I was so distraught I couldn't think straight. As I struggled for words, there was a sudden pounding on the door.

BOOM! BOOM! BOOM!

When I opened the door, three policemen stood outside with weapons drawn.

Uh oh! This is not good. This is not good AT ALL.

The cop in front pushed the door open and asked what was going on. Apparently our fight was so bad the police received numerous complaints from neighbors. As they stepped inside our dark home I pointed at Jerry and said, "We're fighting because he won't help me take care of our son. He refuses to get a job." They asked where our child was and I nodded towards the back bedroom. I told them he was only a few months old and I couldn't make ends meet by myself. No doubt the reek of marijuana lingered in the air. The cops seemed suspicious and diligent to uncover the full truth.

One of the policemen got right in my face and yelled, "Ma'am, even if this loser doesn't do the right thing, you still have to. Do you understand? We could take your child right now and put him into protective care. Do you want that to happen? Do you really want to lose your son? We don't take situations like this very lightly!"

With a renewed vigor and determination to do the right thing, I responded, "I understand completely. I will do whatever I need to do. In fact, I'm taking my son to a safe place right now. I promise."

The cop made it very clear to me if they got one more call things would not go well for us. That was a risk I was not about to take.

When the uniformed men finally left our home, I looked at Jerry. I was just about to ask what he planned to do when, out of the corner of my eye, I noticed a cabinet door that was slightly ajar in the corner of the room. I ran over and looked inside. There were several large bags of marijuana and a bag of cocaine. If the cops had noticed it we would have both been arrested for possession and distribution.

I worried that the policemen were going to get a search warrant and come back. The enormity of the moment blindsided me with horror unlike anything I had ever experienced before. This was not just a close call. It was a wake-up call!

I can't wait on Jerry anymore. I have to do the right thing. I have to do the right thing RIGHT NOW!

I grabbed the bag of cocaine from the cabinet, walked into the bathroom, and flushed it down the toilet without pause. This fueled Jerry's anger towards me, and he began to yell at me again.

Oh no! I can't get into another fight. I will lose my son and go to jail. I have to get out of here right now. Right this minute. Go! Go! Go! Run for your life!

CHAPTER SEVENTEEN

Relinquishing the Reins

THE THREAT OF LOSING MY SON evoked a desperation and fear in me unlike anything else I had ever experienced. The instinct to protect him demanded an immediate response to eliminate all risk of separation. While looking into his beautiful innocent face, I made the decision to call my parents for help. It was my only choice. I had exhausted every other possible option. I knew I couldn't keep him safe in the volatile situation we were in. I had to humble myself and do whatever needed to be done—just as I promised.

I frantically rummaged through several dresser drawers until I found a quarter. Then I quietly snuck out to make the call as quickly as possible before London woke up, or Jerry figured out what I was doing. I had a short one mile jog to the nearest pay phone. On the way, I rehearsed my words and hoped my parents would answer the call. It was only six o'clock in the morning so I assumed they were still asleep.

When I arrived at the phone, I took a deep breath and

told myself, "You've got to do this. It's the right thing to do." As I heard the quarter clank its way into the phone to activate a connection, my heart pounded furiously. I held the receiver to my ear and nervously waited as the phone rang several times.

Please pick up the phone. Please pick up the phone! I don't know what else to do! Please pick up the phone!

Finally, my mother answered with a groggy, "Hello?" I immediately responded with a desperate plea, "Mom, it's me. I need you to come get me and London. Right now. Can you come? Please?" She sounded concerned and startled, as she tried to wake up enough to comprehend my request. She mumbled, "Yes, I can. It's so early. Jen, what's wrong? When do you want me to come?"

I didn't have time to explain. I was too anxious to get back home to London. I was afraid if I stayed on the phone too much longer then something bad would happen. I was also concerned the cops were coming back. The amount of drugs that were still in my house was enough to put me in prison for decades. It was a life or death moment, and there was no time to chat. Through streaming tears I begged, "Just come now, right now! I'll explain when you get here. Hurry, please! As fast as you can!"

In that moment, I empathized with my mother for the first time in my life. I realized she was just as desperate to protect me, as I was my son. I finally understood why she grieved over me the way she had for so long and why she was so desperate to keep me safe. For twenty-four years I had misunderstood everything she tried to do to help me. The epiphany was like a giant spotlight that gave sudden clarity to a lifetime of misperceptions.

I was overcome with love for my mother. Her willingness to swoop into action and do anything she could to help, no matter what time of day, was something nobody else in the world could offer. I was embarrassed that it took so much hardship before I finally understood that she really did love me.

I ran back to get London as fast as I could. Once there, I quickly packed a small bag that contained a few pair of clothes and diapers. It wasn't much. I continued to encourage myself to follow through.

You have to do this. It's the right thing to do. You need to keep London safe.

When my parents finally pulled in, I took a deep breath and approached Jerry while I held London and the bag tightly in my arms. I said, "I can't take care of you *and* London. I really wish things had turned out differently." Then I walked out.

As London and I drove away with my parents I felt both sad and relieved. My life hadn't turned out how I wanted. I wasn't getting married or living happily ever after. Instead, I was a single mother who was scared, broke, and desperate. My decision to leave Jerry was the right one to make, but it was still extremely painful.

A few hours later, after I unpacked and settled into my parent's home, my mother asked if I'd go with her to visit her friend Judy. I had known Judy, and her family, for years because my brother and her son had been best friends since second grade. Our families had developed a close bond through their friendship.

I liked Judy but always perceived her to be one of the shiny, happy Christians who did everything right. She constantly praised God and was always quick to share Bible verses with anyone she encountered. She bubbled over with passion for Christ. So, needless to say, I was uncomfortable about seeing her. The sweet gooey goodness that poured out of her was intimidating to me. I assumed she and my mother wanted to make me feel guilty about everything that had happened. But, I agreed to go anyways because I couldn't bring myself to argue with my mother after everything she had just done to rescue me.

When we arrived at Judy's house, she immediately greeted me with a warm hug and told me how proud she was of me. Her welcome caught me completely off guard.

Proud? Why would she be proud of me?

Her words didn't match my expectations. She didn't ask a lot of questions or interrogate me over the situation either. Rather, she started telling me a story about herself. She said she understood the pain, frustration, and hurt I was going through because she had been through difficult challenges in her life as well. Then she shared the emotional details about an abortion she had when she was about my age.

Whoa! Judy the Christian had an abortion?

My interest was piqued. I hung on every word she said because I was amazed that the joyous, peaceful, encouraging woman I had known for so many years had been through such a horrible, traumatic experience.

Judy explained that despite her guilt, pain, and suffering, God forgave her when she surrendered her life to Him. Her testimony gave me hope. She said there was nothing I could do to make God stop loving me because Jesus already took my punishment when He died on the cross. She said if I acknowledged my sin, and recognized my need for Him, I would be forgiven. Then I could be restored to God, not because of my own actions or abilities, but because of what Christ already did. In that moment, it all started to make sense.

It's not about how good I am; it's about how good He is! It's not even about me; it's about Him! I get it! I finally see!

My body was covered in goose bumps. My whole life I had only focused on the fact my sin separated me from God and made it impossible for me to enter heaven. And while that statement was true, Judy helped me see that Christ took my sins upon Himself when He was crucified. Because He took on my punishment, I could be set free. Payment for my transgressions had already been made. God, in His infinite wisdom, knew it was impossible for me to live a sinless life which is exactly why He sent Christ to die. She even said God would see me as holy and pure, like Christ is, if I just accepted Him.

Me? Seen as pure? But....

Doubtfully I asked, "You mean I can have a relationship with God, just as I am?"

She said, "Yes! He will help you with everything you need. He wants to carry your burden. Just give your life to Him. He will set you on the right path. You can't be good enough to earn salvation. Just let go. He will transform you when you surrender."

Her words made me cry. They were exactly what I wanted to hear. The love she described was the type of unconditional acceptance I had searched my whole life for.

When she asked again if I wanted to give myself to our merciful and loving God, I enthusiastically said, "Yes! Yes! Absolutely!"

While Judy prayed with me I immediately felt my heavy burden lifted. The weight and shame of my sins were removed from my shoulders. My soul was infused with overwhelming peace, despite my circumstances. It was much better than any high I was used to.

My life was forever changed that day. It was February 19, 1993.

I knew I had a mighty God to pave the way, which allowed me to quit struggling and worrying so much. I rested in His promise to provide. I knew my lifestyle would be completely different than I was used to, and it would be a lot better than relying on myself or anybody else. I told God I accepted His plan for me whatever it was. I was all in.

Even though I began to read the Bible and develop my new relationship with God, I still struggled with feelings of insecurity at times. My mother wanted me to attend church with her on Sundays but I felt awkward about going at first. So many people there knew about my multitude of sins and I was embarrassed. So I stayed home on Sunday mornings and watched Dr. Charles Stanley preach on television. His powerful sermons cut straight to the heart of my tangled emotions. They helped me see myself as God saw me, which instilled the confidence I needed to eventually connect with others.

When I finally got up the nerve to attend a small church for the first time, I was amazed at the welcome I received. Numerous people encouraged me and said they were happy to see me. My allusions about the shiny, happy Christian club were proven wrong once again. The church was not full of people who lived perfect lives but just the opposite. In fact, most of them had stories similar to my own. They had been broken and redeemed just like I was.

I realized that church was a safe place to seek accountability and encouragement with others. As well as learn and grow. Their excitement and zeal for Christ was contagious too. Whenever we sang hymns I remembered from childhood, I couldn't help but cry. I was constantly reminded how good, patient, and merciful God had been with me. I knew I was exactly where I was supposed to be—finally.

A few weeks later I decided to get baptized. I wanted to declare before the congregation that God had answered their prayers for me. When I stood in the water in front of the sanctuary the pastor proclaimed, "We've been waiting for this one a long time, haven't we?" The audience erupted in applause and shouts of amen. I was overwhelmed to see how many people actually cared about me. For almost a decade, dozens of people I didn't even know were asking God to move in my life, and He did! Believe me, I was just as astonished as they were.

After my baptism that afternoon, a large crowd gathered at my parent's house to celebrate even more. They brought food and gifts and continued to encourage me. When a lady told me all the angels in heaven were throwing a party for me, I couldn't help but cry. It made me feel so special to realize that the giant God of the universe knew me by name.

God must have big plans for me. He wouldn't have saved my life so many times or brought me here for no reason. I can hardly wait to see what He does next.

CHAPTER EIGHTEEN

Angel Baby

A FEW WEEKS AFTER London and I moved into my parent's house, Jerry's parents called to see how we were doing. I love his parents tremendously, so I grieved over the possibility of losing them through the difficult situation. Breakups usually divide more people than the two individuals involved. I wanted London to get to know his grandparents on both sides of the family too, so I was excited to hear from them.

Unfortunately, the call didn't go well. His mother asked if I would have phone service turned on for Jerry, so she could remain in communication with him from Florida where she lived. I was shocked by the request. From a mother's point of view, I could understand her desire to stay connected with her son. However, I was unemployed, broke, and had no idea how I was going to even support my own child, much less hers. I declined by saying my priority had to be London, not her twenty-nine year old. I could tell she was disappointed with my response, which broke my heart. Sadly, that was the last time we ever talked.

Much to my surprise, Jerry showed up at my parent's house to see me the next day. I was hopeful that things had turned around for him over the few weeks we had been separated. Optimistically I opened the door with a fluttering heart. That's when I noticed the moving truck parked in the driveway behind him. Instead of coming to reconcile our relationship, he was just letting me know he decided to move to Florida. He only stopped by, briefly, to say goodbye to London.

Jerry's words felt like a jagged sword had been thrust through the middle of my body. Actually, it was worse than that. Not only did I feel the proverbial pain to the gut, it was as if he twisted the dagger to create the most turmoil possible. I could not fathom why he didn't want to stay and be involved in raising our son. He offered no explanation. He held London for a few short minutes then handed him back to me. He left without another word.

We never saw him again. Ever.

Questions have perplexed my mind for years. To this day, I still don't understand why things ended with Jerry the way they did. Of course, I know why I left the horrible environment our son was born into. But I hadn't meant for my son to be fatherless. God knows I prayed many prayers hoping Jerry would come back.

A few weeks after our last goodbyes, my dad was offered a job in Atlanta, Georgia. My parents asked if I was interested in moving with them. I didn't want to leave my childhood stomping grounds. The few good memories I had were playing in the woods behind their house or chasing fireflies at night. However, the opportunity for a fresh start somewhere sounded wonderful. Especially since I was afraid of wandering back into the snare of drugs I had barely escaped. So I decided to go.

A few months later, London and I made the transition to Atlanta. I still struggled to accept the reality of being a single parent. I sent Jerry a letter with my new address and welcomed him to call or visit London whenever he wanted. I never wanted to face the day when London would ask why he didn't have a dad. I knew the only viable answer to give him would be the truth, which would be painful. So I desperately hoped that day would never come.

Despite things not turning out how I wanted, God graciously and abundantly provided for us. We witnessed our heavenly Father intervene in our lives in countless ways. Being completely dependent on nobody but Him was the best thing that happened to us, and we really got to know Him that way.

My relationship with my parents, which had been distant and strained almost my entire life, was radically transformed. I realized that my assumptions about their love being conditional had been terribly wrong. Having a child allowed me to see myself from their perspective. I finally understood why they couldn't condone my reckless lifestyle and relentlessly tried to find help.

I was profoundly grateful my parents still loved me. Despite the stress I had put them through for two and a half decades, their steadfast love never gave up. As many times as I defiantly yelled at them to leave me alone, they never stopped loving me. However, they did lose many nights of sleep and got many gray hairs. The way they received me back home was a perfect picture of how God accepted me: no matter what I had done, our intimacy was restored. To them, their love had never gone away. But for me, I finally felt it and reciprocated.

My parent's provision of a room allowed me to focus on taking care of all the extra attention an infant needs. I developed a close bond with London as he learned to crawl, sit, and say his first words. I cherished every moment that we had together. I knew each day with him was a gift that I never wanted to take for granted.

When London's tiny little baby body took his first steps at seven months old, I thanked God for the opportunity to witness the amazing feat. Who knew I was capable of loving someone so much? The feeling often overtook me in giant waves that were so powerful they shook me to the core. Many times those kind of precious moments took my breath away, which humbled me and kept me grateful to be alive.

Being a single mother definitely had its challenges, especially for the first few years. London constantly needed new clothes and food. Not to mention, thousands of diapers. He was a very poopy baby! Food stamps and a small welfare check helped a little, but it wasn't enough. I took on every extra job I could find like mowing the neighbor's yard, filing paperwork, stuffing envelopes, and babysitting.

Being poor forced me to find creative ways to entertain London for free. We often built blanket forts with cushions from the couch or old cardboard boxes. We sat inside our makeshift castles and made up stories for each other. Even plain, old sheets of paper took on new life forms when we made hats or folded them into animal shapes for fun. We also went to the toy store, at least twice a week, just to play with the abundance of toys there. Since he didn't have many at home, why not? We spent hours playing with every ball, car, and book that London showed an interest in. He never once threw a tantrum or asked to take the toys home either. I suppose he didn't know people could do that.

For London's first Christmas, we stood in line with hundreds of other poor single mothers at the welfare office. There we received a small box of toys which included a plastic bucket and shovel for playing in the dirt and some coloring books. I was extremely grateful for the gifts but the experience compelled me to work as hard as I could to provide for him myself. I wanted so much more for him than a handout.

Many afternoons were spent in the back yard teaching London to play baseball and basketball. I even started his sports training before he could walk. He was quite good too. He could swing a small plastic bat and hit the ball every time I threw it to him. Then he'd wobble around the bases in the yard while I pretended to chase him. Even his pediatrician noted that he developed physical abilities earlier than most other babies of the same age.

London and I also listened to a lot of music. He seemed to be naturally gifted with an appreciation and connection to melodic sounds. We often jumped on my bed together with the music turned up so loud we could feel the house shake. It was a lot of fun!

When London was eighteen months old, I decided to go back to school. I enrolled in a private art college in Atlanta and transferred most of my credits from MTSU. While I attended class, London went to a daycare program at a church near our home. He loved the social interaction, and the schedule worked out perfectly for both of us. Several teachers told me that London was more expressive than the other children in class and they expected him to be a famous singer or even president one day. I didn't doubt it one bit. I mean, God Himself told me He had big plans, and I wasn't about to doubt Him anymore!

About a year later I finally graduated, summa cum laude, and received my bachelor's degree. It was a proud moment; one I thought had been lost forever. I hoped the accomplishment would land me a better job. I didn't want to work three jobs around the clock like I had done for so many years. So I asked God to provide the perfect opportunity: one that was challenging, used my specific gifts and talents, and provided enough income and benefits to take care of us.

While praying, I began to feel weird. Almost as if God was asking something from me instead. In fact, it felt like He was asking me to trust Him by giving up my welfare and food stamps.

Um, God, I need your help finding a job. Now you're asking me to give up what little money I do have? Can't you help me find a job first?

I was confused. But I couldn't shake the feeling He was trying to stretch my faith. That said, I didn't obey Him immediately. I felt insecure and even doubted my ability to hear God properly. Yet, the more I wrestled with the decision, the more I felt convicted to do as He asked. Remembering all the ways He had miraculously provided for me in the past, I became embarrassed by my doubt and anxiety. So after mocking myself over a lack of courage, I finally cancelled welfare.

Okay God. What are you doing here? Why are you asking me to let go of what little income I have? This goes against all of my paternal instincts. God, I'm scared! I will choose to trust you even though it doesn't feel good. I'm sorry for my doubt and insecurity.

Lo and behold, just a few days later, I was offered a job. It wasn't just any job either. It was work I hadn't even applied for, completely by happenstance. The job met every specific request I had prayed for. I was blown away. God showed up and amazed me again. Why do I ever doubt?

During my first year as a single mother, my relationship with London and God grew to levels I never could have imagined. It was remarkable. However, I knew resentment still lingered in my heart towards Jerry. I often wrestled with unanswered questions about why he didn't want to help or be involved. I constantly wondered if he would ever send financial support or try and connect with London.

When London's first birthday came and went without a word from Jerry, my resentment erupted like an oozing wound. I was consumed with anger and bitterness. I even found it difficult to enjoy London's first big day because of my disappointment.

Later that night, as I lie awake in bed wrestling with animosity, God pressed me to let go of all my unmet expectations and bitterness towards Jerry.

Are you asking me to forgive Jerry? He hasn't even asked! How can I forgive him if he doesn't apologize? He hasn't sent a single dime to help. He hasn't just hurt me; he abandoned his own son!

Deep inside, I knew I wouldn't be able to heal and grow any further if I held onto my resentment. I knew I would be riddled with grief for the rest of my life if I continued to let Jerry disappoint me. Bitterness would ruin my ability to be the best mother I could be for my son.

Lord, this is another burden I need to give you, because it is too heavy for me. I choose to forgive Jerry even though it hurts, even though he hasn't apologized. I need you to be the Father to my son. I need you to protect him and provide for every need throughout his life. I trust you to deal with Jerry however you see fit. Help me focus on you so I can be the best mother I can be. Please heal my wounded heart so that I don't become bitter. I want to trust you without pause. Thank you for everything you have done for us!

Once I prayed, I immediately felt at peace again—just as I had the day I first surrendered my life to God. I obviously needed to relinquish control over to Him again. Acknowledging His ability to defend, protect, and provide was all I needed to do to keep from being paralyzed by worry. It changed my focus from my circumstances to the One who gave me life. God graciously traded my feelings of rejection for peace, joy and strength.

I wish I could say that I never struggled with insecurity, doubt, or fear again, but it wouldn't be true. Oftentimes I worried how my son would turn out, after being raised without a father. I even worried about little things, like teaching him to use the bathroom standing up. It sounds silly, but it really concerned me! I couldn't take him in the women's restroom with me forever, so I worried. Then I worried about sending him into the men's bathroom alone. I even worried when I found him playing in my makeup or wearing my shoes! Despite my ongoing fears, God gave us everything we needed, every step along the way. He even brought male friends into my life at the perfect moments to help with the kind of things I couldn't quite do myself; like picking out the best cup for playing hockey.

When London was three years old, my trust in God was put to the test. Things got extremely challenging as a single parent. London was a very strong and active toddler. Whenever I took him to a restaurant, he climbed out of his chair and hid at the feet of strangers under their table. If I went to a department store, he ran and hid inside the clothes racks where I couldn't reach him. I received thousands of funny glances and comments from strangers as they watched me try and coax my son out of his precarious hiding places all over town. Their mumbles and critical judgment made me feel embarrassed and incompetent as a mother.

One day when I took London to the grocery store, he climbed out of the buggy while my back was turned. Then he took off running. His strong little legs maneuvered his tiny body through the store, around carts, and down aisles much faster than I could go. Whenever I called his name, he laughed and ran even harder. I guess he thought our chase was a game, like we played at home. However, I was gripped with fear that he would get hurt or lost.

The pursuit seemed to last forever as I dodged displays and shopping carts and curious onlookers to try and catch him. Then, without a care or concern in the world, he ignorantly ran right out the front sliding door and into the parking lot. Panic consumed me as I ran after him. I yelled at other customers to stop the running toddler, but he was too quick for anybody's grasp.

After an exhaustive and nerve-racking chase across a lane of traffic, I finally caught up to him on the other side of the parking lot, in between parked cars. I grabbed him by the shirt and hugged him tightly as I gasped for air. Relief flooded my being but I was completely distraught. I demanded he never run away from me again while tears ran down my face. I was grateful he wasn't hurt but angry that his recklessness could have cost him his life. My anxious demeanor frightened him and he started crying too.

Because London lacked much life experience, he didn't understand that he had done something wrong. I knew that my rules were meant to keep him safe, because I loved him so much. But he thought I wasn't allowing him to have any fun. For the first time, I felt a wedge come between us that broke my heart.

In that moment, God helped me realize that His boundaries were for the same reasons. My limited perspective doesn't allow me to see the big picture like He does. His rules were really for my good, to keep me safe, because of how much He loves me.

God also reminded me of all the times I ran and hid from Him, and how He patiently waited for me. Despite my recklessness, He embraced me with loving arms. I realized how much my own careless actions throughout life had hurt those who loved me. Again, I grieved for the way I had misunderstood my parents for so many years.

As London grew up, anytime he made bad decisions that required discipline I had to reach out for God's help. It was easy to spank him or slap his hand as a toddler, as a warning to stop doing something. But, once he was about six years old it just wasn't effective. Plus, I wanted to teach him *why* things were wrong. I never wanted him to be confused like I was as a kid. So I depended on God for clever ideas to help me.

For example, one day after London played with the kids

next door, their mother came over to talk with me. She wasn't happy. She stood on my front porch with two crying children and accused London of stealing Pokémon cards from their collection. Now, I knew London loved Pokémon because he had a collection of his own. I even helped him organize his cards into a binder, so I knew exactly which ones he owned. I assured the mother I would look into it and return any ill-begotten items if they were found.

When I opened London's notebook, sure enough, he had the cards they claimed he had taken. I was hoping it wouldn't be true. It grieved me to bring any sort of discipline onto my child. Regardless, he needed to learn.

I tried to spank London with my hand but could never find it in me to hit him very hard. His cute little face just smiled back at me and said, "That wasn't so bad." Trying hard not to smile, I said, "London, unfortunately your punishment is not over. I need you to understand why stealing is wrong."

Oh God, help me. I don't know how to do this. I can't spank him any harder. I just can't. I don't have it in me. What should I do?

I suddenly had an idea. I picked up London's binder, grabbed him by the hand, and we walked next door to see the kids he had stolen from. When we got there, I told the kids they could pick out any cards they wanted from London's collection. They were thrilled! They flipped through every page and took several that interested them. London was devastated as they danced around in happy jubilee with their new cards. They had chosen his very favorite ones. He experienced firsthand what it felt like having something stolen from him.

That punishment was hard for both of us. It killed me to

see him hurt. However, he immediately understood why the crime was wrong. In fact, he still refers to that day as one of his greatest life lessons. See, even when I felt incompetent as a parent and unsure of how to discipline a rambunctious toddler of my own, God came through with great wisdom.

London and I have been through a lot together. Despite my failures and insecurities along the way, I've been blessed. Today London is quite accomplished at songwriting, singing, recording, and playing the guitar. In fact, he even leads worship at church. How incredible is that? When God said He had plans, He wasn't kidding!

There have only been a few times that London ever asked about his father. I simply answered every question the best I could. Fortunately, they were simple questions like what color are his eyes? I'm sure he's wrestled with more than that, but he never focused on what or who he didn't have. Rather, he's always made the most of what he did have.

When London was baptized in front of our church at nineteen years old, he shared a beautiful testimony about being raised by his heavenly father. He made a room full of people cry. Despite the unbelievable challenges we faced when he was born, he has thrived and become an incredible young man. He's sweet, loyal, caring, protective, and affectionate. All the qualities he missed from an earthly father, God miraculously provided in abundance to him. It's amazing!

My nickname for London has always been Angel Baby. That's because he was a gift straight from heaven. I have learned more about the meaning of life through Angel Baby, than any teacher, pastor, book, or sermon on earth. Since God entrusted him into my care, I never took my role as his mother lightly. It was a role I certainly didn't deserve, or even knew how to perform. But if the Creator of the universe felt I was the right person to raise him, then I depended on Him for instructions along the way. That strategy seems to have worked out pretty well.

CHAPTER NINETEEN

Life Lessons Learned

I'VE LEARNED A LOT of valuable life lessons. Granted, most of them were learned the hard way—through trials, traumas, and tragedy—but they were all experiences God used to transform me into who I am today. Jesus brought me through serious pain, hurt, abuse, addiction, disability, depravity, and destitution. He then carried me to a place of comfort, joy, peace, purpose, and eternal life. God, in His infinite wisdom and grace, showed up and did something amazing with all the shattered pieces of my brokenness. He didn't always move in ways I expected, but His plans definitely turned out better than my own.

Having sensory processing disorder was a mysterious problem I wrestled with throughout my entire life. Because my parents were unaware that the condition even existed, it caused them to make a lot of incorrect assumptions. They, and others, thought I was a cranky, ornery, rambunctious kid. I suppose that's true to some level. However, our lack of knowledge regarding the disorder set the stage for disaster. It created a world of misunderstanding from everyone's perspective.

The torment I experience with sensory overload is very real to me even though it appears to be senseless to others. From my perspective, every time my parents and I fought over a scratchy dress or tight shoes, I assumed they hated me and purposefully wanted me to suffer. Of course, now I know that wasn't true at all. One reason I've written this memoir is to help people understand how the world looks and feels to someone with SPD. It's very different from the way I assume others perceive it.

I believe discipline and boundaries for children are important, but it's critical to find ways to communicate that's instructive, encouraging, and helps them learn. My parents struggled at times with consistency and unity between themselves while they endlessly searched for a technique that worked with me. It was especially difficult because the lines were blurred between problems related to my disorder and truly defiant behavior. Therefore, I was almost always in trouble, whether I deserved it or not. The times my parents calmly and gently explained *why* I was in trouble were the times I learned the most.

The best thing my parents ever did was not giving up on me. Even when their attempts to get through to me failed, they never stopped praying for me. Even when I pushed them away and screamed how much I hated them, they never stopped pursuing a relationship with me. There were many times they had to make tough decisions not to enable my reckless lifestyle and bad decisions. My response to their healthy actions strained our relationship at the time, but there's no doubt now that they did the right thing. If they had bailed me out when my life was out of control, then I never would have learned to seek God and become dependent on Him. So while I may have felt abandoned by them at the time, I'm grateful they practiced tough love like they did.

The good news is we have a powerful God who is in the business of restoring relationships. The first twenty-four years of my life with my parents were marked by chaos, turmoil, pain, and suffering. But the last twenty have been an amazing process of healing, reconciliation, and complete restoration. I love my parents more than I ever thought possible. We are very close today. When God allowed me to have a son of my own, I gained an enormous amount of respect for them. I realized that my parents loved me so much they would have given their lives to save me if that would have worked. Fortunately, Christ did that for them.

Over and above everything else, sin was my biggest problem. It disguised itself as pleasure and made me believe it was innocent fun. See, sin is a hideous monster that lurks in the shadows, ready to devour apathetic victims. Once I allowed it into my life, I became prideful and arrogant believing I was clever and strong enough to handle it. Boy was I wrong. My life spiraled completely out of control while I wandered aimlessly down a path that was meant to annihilate me forever. I never could have won the battle with sin by myself. Fortunately, the same power that allowed Jesus to walk on water and rise again from the dead was the same power God used to transform my life.

God is who I need to be unified with first and foremost. I realized that after multiple broken relationships. I cannot be a good mother, sister, daughter, or wife one day if I am not in regular communion with God. It's because of my intimacy with Him that I am enabled to love others properly.

Searching for people that could make me feel significant was also a fruitless endeavor. Assuming true love meant someone who allowed me to get away with bad habits was a huge lie that I believed. The people who truly loved me were the ones who wanted what was best for me even if that meant confronting me with something I didn't want to hear.

I used to see myself as a wounded, hurt, disabled little girl with a lot of emotional baggage. Life seemed cruel and unfair. I trusted no one. However, God used every single trial, tragedy, and disappointment in my life to develop character, stamina, perseverance, and integrity. Now, I'm prepared for future battles as a warrior princess!

The Creator of the universe knows all of us by name. He was able to orchestrate hundreds of people and events throughout my life to bring me into relationship with Himself. That's pretty amazing! Because I had serious addictions, I experienced God as a miraculous healer. Because I was abused, hurt, mocked, slandered, and taken advantage of, I watched God defend, protect, and vindicate me. And because I was so destitute and poor, God proved Himself as an incredible provider. Today, I no longer live as a victim. Instead, I consider it joy to have been through so many various trials. It is through those experiences that I got to know how awesome and powerful He really is!

My biggest misunderstanding growing up was not having a clear understanding of who God really is. I struggled to trust Him because I didn't know Him. Once I got to know Him, the more I wanted Him in my life. The more relationship grew, the deeper I fell in love with Him. This wellspring of life made it easier to trust God and follow His lead. God is who He says He is which is awesome!

Throughout my life, hardships have never disappeared. The desire to use drugs and other temptations can still annoy me from time to time. As long as I'm in this world, in my weak earthly body, I'm going to wrestle with sin and temptation. The difference is I have access to the One who understands and can enable me to overcome. I've been drug free for over twenty years now.

To live in victory means to rely on Christ every step of the way. When I feel entitled to sin, I do. When I feel grateful for God's mercy and grace, I don't. When I understand how loving He is, I want to help others know Him.

Being involved at a good church has helped me grow by leaps and bounds. It's an incredible source of rejuvenation, accountability, encouragement, and teaching. When I'm active with a body of believers who love God, then I have a lot more courage to navigate life's bumpy road. I'm so thankful God surrounded me with a spiritual family who motivate me to deepen my faith.

Obedience never comes easy. It's not something I've ever been able to do in my own strength. The key is reliance upon Christ. The more I stay in a place of humility and gratitude for everything He's done, the easier it becomes. The more He's the center of my life, the more the desires of my heart are in line with His.

God has given me indescribable peace despite my past circumstances. There is no chemical that compares to the pure joy that comes from an intimate relationship with Him. Watching Him work out the details of my life has given me confidence to trust Him with everything. That includes my health, relationships, career, and even my finances.

I believe my time, talents, and resources are gifts from God. Therefore, it's my responsibility to manage what He's given me with excellence. The Bible is a great instruction manual too! My role is simply to use what He's given me to glorify Him and help others know Him.

When someone places their life into God's hands, they are eternally secure. There is nothing anybody can do to cause them to lose their salvation. Be warned though, there is still an evil enemy who seeks to destroy those of us who love God. Because Satan cannot have my soul, he would love to ruin my testimony or prevent me from helping others know the Truth. However, I can be confident and sleep at night knowing God has my back: and front and sides and above and below and before and after and in between.

I still struggle with sensory processing disorder, but I'm in the process of learning why God has allowed me to have such a difficult condition. I know He could heal me if He wanted to. So why hasn't He? When I am weak, He is strong. It sounds like an old cliché or just some line from a children's song, but it's true. He demonstrates His strength and power through my weaknesses. That way He gets the glory, praise, and worship. Not me. He allows no room for me to boast or have confidence in my own abilities. It keeps me humble and dependent. Besides, there's no telling how much of a mess I would make of things if I weren't desperately relying on Him.

God always had a plan for me, since before I was even born. My life came full circle when God called me into prison ministry. Relating to prisoners is easy for me because I am very familiar with hurt, anger, and rejection like many of them. I'm also quite experienced at making bad decisions like stealing, trespassing, and selling drugs. It is only by God's grace and mercy that I am alive and not behind bars myself, so I feel compelled to use my freedom to help.

I want others to know there is hope and forgiveness for them, no matter what they've done. However, when I first got involved with prison ministry, I never expected the life-changing impact it would have on me as well. At first, I was nervous, scared, and unsure of finding the right words to say. Nonetheless, my faith was radically boosted when I followed God's call to serve.

Imagine this: you wake up one day and never get to see your friends or family again for the rest of your life. Imagine never holding your children or even knowing where they are. Imagine physical wounds so deep and numerous that your entire body is a canvas of brutal scars. Those are just a few of the real stories of inmates I've talked to.

Many prisoners I've met are at the beginning of lifelong sentences with no hope for a future. They know they'll be staring at the same gray walls for years and years to come. They've literally lost everything they had, and for a few that includes their own children. A night sky full of stars, sitting under a tree, or splashing around in the ocean will become distant memories. Most of them are devastated by their loss and consumed with grief.

Other inmates I've met have done their time and are about to be released. Surprisingly, rather than being excited about their pending freedom, they are oftentimes nervous and insecure. Many of them have nowhere to go. Their families and friends have shunned them. Finding a job, a place to live, and a community of safe people that will give them a chance are gigantic obstacles they must overcome. The odds really are stacked against them. If anybody needs the Creator to move mountains in their life, it's them!

Jessica was the first inmate I met inside a maximum-security prison. She was withdrawn and appeared to have the weight of the world on her shoulders. When I first noticed her, she sat alone in the room full of prisoners as she mumbled self-condemning accusations to herself. She never even raised her eyes from the ground. I watched her for several minutes and felt like God was moving me to speak with her. Something about her mannerisms reminded me of myself. His prompting made me nervous, so I quickly prayed, "Okay God, I need you to show up now, because that girl is obviously hurting. You need to bring the right words to me if I go over there."

As I approached Jessica I simply asked, "Would you like to talk?" She barely raised her face to see me. Through a painful grimace she nodded yes. I began by telling her who Christ is and how He died for her sins. No matter what crimes she had committed, He wanted a relationship with her. I shared how He miraculous intervened in my own life, despite many stupid things I had done. She was visibly shaken. Tears streamed down her face in bucket loads while I talked.

Through heaving and tears she tried to share parts of her story with me. She was only twenty-six years old and had recently been sentenced for life. Regret was eating her alive. She told me about her beautiful six-year-old daughter, who she missed terribly. She had not been able to touch her since she had been arrested. At that moment, I remembered my own encounter with the police and the threat of losing my son. My heart broke for her.

As Jessica continued to sob, I started sharing God's

character attributes with her. I said, "He is powerful. He is a provider. He can transform you. He can heal, vindicate, defend, and protect you! He can turn ALL things around for your good and His glory. Though you have consequences because of things you've done, He is still on the throne! He is in the business of restoring relationships! He loves and adores you so much. His one and only Son paid the death penalty for you, so that you could live in freedom for all eternity in heaven. Your situation may feel impossible to you, but it's not impossible for God!"

After several moments of declaring His love for her, I finally asked, "Would you like to have a relationship with Christ? He sent me all the way in here just to tell you how much He loves you!"

At that point her eyes finally met mine. One side of her mouth slightly curled into a tiny smile and she gently whispered, "Yes."

Jessica and I immediately prayed together. I had the awesome privilege of hearing her apologize for her sins and surrender her life to Christ. I was so excited I could hardly contain my joy. I jumped up from my seat and gave her a high five which actually made her laugh. Then I said, "Woo-hoo! All of heaven is having a party on your behalf. Welcome to the family. This is cause for celebration!"

My happy dance was cut short. Jessica started bawling again. The gravity of her consequences was still too much for her to bear, so I shifted gears in our conversation. For the next few minutes I focused on telling her how Christ saw her. I said, "The world may call you names and associate you with your past crimes. However, God sees you as pure and righteous because of what Christ did. You are a new creature in Him. Your eternal life in heaven is secure, no matter what happens here on earth. God has a plan for you. He can use you, despite your circumstances. I know this firsthand! He can even restore your relationship with your daughter. He has the power to transform everything in your life, no matter what obstacles the world puts in front of you. You are not your sin!"

Jessica's face lit up again, and this time a huge smile grew on her face behind her swollen red eyes. Her countenance completely changed. I got to witness the devastating burden of sin physically lift from her shoulders. The worried strain on her face turned into joy, as she found confidence to face the rocky road ahead. She easily thanked me a hundred times for telling her things that she had never heard before.

When I got home that night, I researched Jessica's crimes online. I found numerous newspaper articles that depicted the gruesome details of the pointless murder she had committed with her boyfriend, just to get their hands on some money. I even found her personal Facebook page which was full of cute pictures of her playing with her daughter just like any other young mother, up until the day she was arrested.

I broke down and cried uncontrollably for several hours. I knew God had rescued me from a lot. I knew He was gracious. But that day, I experienced a whole new depth to His mercy and love. It completely overwhelmed me, and it was quite remarkable. Not to mention it was pretty amazing how He allowed me, a rambunctious kid with a tangled up past, to help someone else that desperately needed Him. I was blown away.

Albeit not many, there were a few good decisions I did make in life like having my son. I'm eternally grateful I didn't lose him during childbirth, or by going to prison, or by letting anybody convince me I shouldn't have him. He is a precious gift from God. I grieve for women who believe there's no hope and choose to abort. Adoption is always an option for those who don't have the support they need to raise a child alone. In fact, my best friend Tricia adopted four children. Those kids have thrived since they joined her family and a home full of love and care.

I fully expect the rest of my life will be as full of adventure and amazing stories as the first half. One thing is for certain though. I no longer wrestle with all those perplexing questions that plagued my mind for so long.

Why would a loving God allow me to go through so many difficult situations? Can a perfect, holy God forgive me of the innumerable bad things I have done? Why was I created with such a bizarre disorder? What is my purpose for being here?

I believe God placed all of us into this crazy world together—not by happenstance or coincidence—but lovingly and strategically. We were created for a relationship with Him and each other in order to impact the world around us for good. He will go to any lengths necessary to have a relationship with us because His love is so intense. He's jealous of anything that takes our hearts and minds away from Him.

Nothing is impossible for God. He never once abandoned me or turned a blind eye when I was going through various trials in my life. He allowed them to happen for a reason. God uses me all the time now to help and encourage other people which is nothing short of miraculous!

I've also seen His plan for my son unfold in truly amazing ways. Watching my Angel Baby lead worship is proof that God can turn all things around!

See, God had a master plan all along—for such a time as this. Instead of wrestling over how, what, or why I am here, I can joyfully and confidently respond to Him with one simple word now: YES!

Here I am with Mom and Dad a few months after I was born.

I always have the same grumpy look on my face whenever Mom
makes me pose in a dress.

Rodney and me in 1970.
What a rambunctious
smirk!

These are my wonderful, inspiring grandparents.
Papa and Mamaw Mills (from Florida) are on the left.
Papa and Mamaw Allison (from Alabama) are on the right.

Rodney and I were lucky to have Santa visit us at home every year. I'm excited because I'm about to ask him for a drum set, again.

My brother and I were always goofing around.

Rodney, Debbie and me in 1985.

Here's my family at Rodney's wedding. My dad was battling cancer, and I was a few months pregnant.

Angel Baby and me when he was six months old.

Mother and son, all grown up.

ACKNOWLEDGEMENTS

I would like to acknowledge all my friends who helped put this book together. First, I owe much thanks to Kevin Cross and Steven White. Their generous encouragement inspired me to start writing in the first place. Randy Thomas helped me structure my stories in a way they would make sense to people who aren't inside my head. Likewise, Rebecca Anaya did an amazing job copyediting. Without them this book would be full of rambling thoughts, grammatical errors and typos. I'm also grateful for the talented Beth VanDyke. She did an incredible job designing the cover.

I'd also like to thank all my childhood friends in Tennessee. They were there for me when I was lost, confused, broken, ashamed, confused, hurt and rejected. They constantly made me laugh and smile, despite the war I had raging on the inside. They loved me unconditionally and I'm grateful for their continued friendship.

Lastly, I must thank Angel Baby. He is a blessing for sure. I couldn't be any prouder of the amazing young man he has grown up to be. God was right, He had a plan for us all along.

ABOUT JENNIFER LEIGH ALLISON

Jennifer Leigh Allison currently resides in Atlanta, Georgia with her son, London. She frequently volunteers with prison ministry events around the Southeast and loves sharing her testimony at speaking engagements.

You can connect with Jennifer online at:

Blog - jenniferleighallison.com

Facebook - facebook.com/jenniferleighallison

Twitter - @KidRambunctious

35978796R00146

Made in the USA
Lexington, KY
01 October 2014